C00 19246080

EDINBURGH CITY LIBRARIES

D0232240

A43

NEWINGTON DIVISION

LOC.		
DATE		

CASSEROLES

EDINBURGH
CITY
LIBRARIES

RYLAND
PETERS
& SMALL

LONDON NEW YORK

CASSEROLES
FROM TAGINE TO COQ AU VIN

Sonia Stevenson

photography by **William Lingwood**

EDINBURGH
CITY
LIBRARIES

Senior Designer Steve Painter
Commissioning Editor Elsa Petersen-Schepelern
Indexer Hilary Bird
Production Meryl Silbert
Art Director Gabriella Le Grazie
Publishing Director Alison Starling

Food Stylist Julz Beresford
Assistant Food Stylist Christine Rodrigues
Stylist Antonia Gaunt
Photographer's Assistant Emma Bentham-Wood

First published in Great Britain in 2001
by Ryland Peters & Small
Kirkman House
12–14 Whitfield Street
London W1T 2RP
www.rylandpeters.com

Text © Sonia Stevenson 2001
Design and photographs
© Ryland Peters & Small 2001

Printed in China

The author's moral rights have been asserted. All
rights reserved. No part of this publication may be
reproduced, stored in a retrieval system or
transmitted in any form or by any means, electronic,
mechanical, photocopying or otherwise, without the
prior permission of the publisher.

10 9 8 7 6 5 4 3 2 1

ISBN 1 84172 195 6

A CIP record for this book is available from
the British Library.

For Patrick and Seren,
my Oldest and Youngest in the Family.

Author's acknowledgements

I am deeply grateful to Kai Wood and Sue, his wife,
for their help with the Chinese recipes; to Luc Votan,
for his assistance with Vietnamese and other dishes
from South-east Asia; to my sister and brother-in-law
Gillian and Brenton Creelman in America, for their
help and patience; and last but certainly not least to
Elsa, my editor, for trying to keep me on the straight
and narrow and being an ever-ready source of help in
Times of Trouble.

Acknowledgements

Our thanks for the beautiful props to Cucina Direct,
whose products are available by mail order, and via
www.cucinadirect.com.

Notes

All spoon measurements are level.

Fresh herbs are used in this book unless otherwise
stated. If using dried herbs, halve the quantity given.

Unsalted butter has been used in all the recipes. If
using salted butter, add a little less salt to the dish.

Uncooked or partly cooked eggs should not be
served to the very old or frail, the very young or to
pregnant women.

The oven should be preheated to the specified
temperature, except where indicated otherwise.

0206   31 OCT 2001

EDINBURGH CITY LIBRARIES AND INFORMATION SERVICES	AC C0019246080		CL TX 693
	LO NT	V CYP 01/41	PR £16.99

hJ

contents

The Casserole ...

No other word has ever been used to describe such a diverse variety of dishes. Try to define it in a few words and the explanation simply becomes longer and full of exceptions. It conjures up meat dishes, vegetable dishes, fish dishes, slow cooked dishes, last-minute put-together dishes, gratins, curries, soups, modern dishes, old fashioned traditional recipes and so on. But they do have one thing in common. They are cooked in a simple heatproof dish which could be called a casserole, even if it really is a tagine, hotpot, sandpot or a daube – according to the part of the world in which you live.

As all these names suggest, there are many ways to cook a casserole, but most can be categorized by the technique used to make them.

A ragout is a basic stew with roux-thickened gravy. It comes in two forms, white and brown. White ones have white stock and meat and vegetables sautéed in hot butter without browning. Brown ones have meat and vegetables browned in fat, then flour is added and browned and the dish is then simmered in brown stock. In both cases, the cooking is long and slow and the vegetables are strained out and replaced with new ones as garnishes.

A fricassée is almost the same dish as a white ragout, but here the meat does not require long cooking and so any vegetables are served with the meat, while the gravy is often no more than a light, binding sauce. Egg yolks or arrowroot are often used as liaisons to thicken the sauce.

Braising is reserved for a joint or a large cut of meat or whole chicken. The meat is browned in fat, a little liquid is added and the whole is lidded and sealed to prevent any steam escaping. Slow cooking is essential to prevent drying out and subsequent scorching. The American pot roast, some versions of the Indian *dum pukht* and the French daube are good examples.

The poaching technique can be seen in fish stews of all kinds and many curries, especially those containing coconut milk or yoghurt, which curdle when boiled. But perhaps the most famous of all are the *Poule au Pot*, Chinese red-cooked dishes, *Pot au Feu* or New England Boiled Dinner. The surface is skimmed from time to time and no thickening is used. The result is a dish of extraordinary tenderness.

In America, a casserole is sometimes understood to be an assembly of cooked or part-cooked food baked in an open dish topped with crumbs or herbs, as in the Corn and Scallop Casserole (page 19), the Provençal Tian (page 71) or the Etouffée (page 16) – a cousin, perhaps, of the cassoulet. It is what, in other countries, might be called a 'gratin'.

So – in this exploration of the casseroles of the world, I've discovered that one cook's tagine is another's gumbo; one cook's braise is another's curry. Their similarities are just as exciting as their differences. There are many more marvellous dishes that could have been included, but these are my favourites.

'The history of every nation lies visible on its table.' Nowhere is this quotation from one of Robert Carrier's books more true than of America. It is a potpourri of dishes gleaned from the many cultures of its peoples, made with a cornucopia of ingredients produced by the world's most efficient agricultural system.

In America, it is said, you can get food from any part of the world, any time – either the authentic version, or its truly American descendant.

You want Italian? You have Cioppino – the famous fish stew invented in America by Italian-American fishing communities in California. It is endlessly adaptable, like similar seafood dishes anywhere.

You want French? America's great French cuisines are Creole and Cajun; the first a more sophisticated, city-based style of cooking, the second exuberant country food, both with echoes of African and Spanish influences. Gumbo, for instance, is named after the African word for 'okra'. There are many variations; made with chicken, seafood, duck, greens – and with or without the okra that gave it its name.

Probably one of the most famous American casseroles is Brunswick Stew, cooked in quantity for community gatherings for generations. Originally it included squirrel – and sometimes still does – but now is mostly made with chicken or rabbit. However, most casseroles – the braises, curries, ragouts and stews in other sections of this book – have their American counterparts. There are just a few examples in this chapter. Try to discover more – they are inspiring.

THE AMERICAS

Cioppino

Versions of Cioppino are found all along the West Coast of America, wherever Italians settled: many have been fishermen there for generations. Most recipes seem to agree on one point: you must use a red wine. Some recipes use only shellfish and others insist on using only whole fish, with nothing filleted. However, the majority leave it to you to choose what's best locally.

To make the sauce, heat the olive oil in a large frying pan, then add the onion, garlic, chillies, if using, and the chopped pepper. Sauté gently until softened but not browned, about 10 minutes. Add the wine, bring to the boil and boil until the liquid is reduced to about 100 ml. Put the tomatoes in a blender and purée well. Transfer to the pan, then add the tomato juice, fish stock or clam juice, salt, pepper and fennel seeds. Bring to the boil again, reduce the heat and simmer for 40 minutes.

Meanwhile, brush a large casserole with a thin coating of oil, then add the fish, cover with the boiling red wine sauce and transfer to a preheated oven at 180°C (350°F) Gas 4 for about 15 minutes.

Remove from the oven and add the clams, prawns, herbs and a dash of Tabasco. Cover with a lid or foil and return to the oven for 10 minutes, or until all the shells have opened and the scallops are opaque. Very gently mix the fishes together.

Alternatively, cook the shellfish separately and fold them in after the fish has cooked, rejecting any that have not opened. Serve in large soup plates with plenty of hot garlic buttered baguettes – and finger bowls.

Variations Instead of the seafood, use 250 g ling or halibut, 250 g peeled and deveined prawns, 250 g mussels, 500 g clams, 250 g cooked crab and 250 g scallops.

Alternatively, substitute 125 g fish such as halibut, 500 g prawns, 500 g mussels, 500 g clams, about 24 limpets, 8 pieces of octopus, 8 small scallops and 250 g crab pieces.

Note Make sure all the mussels have been scraped and rinsed, with the beards pulled away and discarded before cooking. Tap them against the kitchen counter and discard any that don't close. Clams should also close when tapped.

500 g white fish such as ling tail fillet or halibut, cut into about 8 chunks

about 500 g clams or a mix of clams and mussels, rinsed and debearded

about 250 g uncooked prawns, peeled and deveined but with tail fins intact

12 scallops, halved crossways

2 tablespoons chopped fresh flat leaf parsley

2 tablespoons chopped fresh coriander or basil

a dash of Tabasco sauce

RED WINE SAUCE

6 tablespoons olive oil

1 large onion, chopped

2 garlic cloves, crushed

2 jalapeño chillies, chopped (optional)

1 red or orange pepper, halved, deseeded and chopped

500 ml red wine

6 ripe tomatoes, skinned, deseeded and chopped

500 ml tomato juice

150 ml fish stock (page 140) or clam juice

1 teaspoon sea salt

¼ teaspoon freshly ground black pepper

¼ teaspoon fennel seeds

SERVES 4

Shrimp and Okra Gumbo

Gumbos are true Creole cooking: their main characteristic is that the flour is always browned slowly to a chestnut colour – a roux. As the word gumbo means 'okra' in Africa, you would think that it should always include that vegetable. Well, some do and some don't – and this one 'do'. Originally gumbo was a Lenten dish, without even the shellfish, but later fish and seafood were added and sometimes chicken too. This was served at a later meal, but left a delicious taste in the stock. Prawns are called 'shrimp' in American English, whatever their size.

Shrimp and Okra Gumbo
step-by-step

1 bunch of watercress, washed and trimmed

1 bunch of parsley, washed and trimmed

1 bunch of spinach, washed and trimmed

10 spring onions, green ends only

1 bunch of chard or beet greens, washed and trimmed

500 g uncooked, unpeeled prawns (shrimp)

1 litre chicken stock (page 134) or water

1 sprig of thyme

1 sprig of marjoram

2 bay leaves

5 whole allspice berries

1½ tablespoons butter or peanut oil

2 tablespoons plain flour

2 garlic cloves, crushed

1 onion, chopped

½ teaspoon cayenne pepper

4 crab claws, preferably uncooked

250 g Creole smoked garlic sausage (andouille) or Polish sausage, cut into 1 cm slices (optional)

2–3 dozen clams and/or mussels, well scrubbed and debearded if necessary

8–12 medium okra

1 teaspoon Tabasco sauce

SERVES 4

1 Pour 500 ml lightly salted water into a large saucepan and bring to the boil. Press in the watercress, parsley, spinach, spring onions and chard or beet greens. Cover and cook until just tender, about 5 minutes. Strain through a colander, reserving the cooking water. Chop the greens and set aside.

2 To make the stock, peel the prawns and put the shells and heads, if any, into a large saucepan or casserole dish. Add the reserved cooking water, stock or water, thyme, marjoram, bay leaves and allspice. Simmer for 15 minutes and set aside.

6 Add the crab claws to the casserole, then add the reserved hot stock. Add the sausage, if using. Bring to the boil.

7 Add the clams, return to the boil, then simmer, covered, for about 15 minutes or until the clams open.

Meanwhile, to prepare the okra, trim minimally around the stalk end, without cutting into the middle.

3 Strain the stock into a saucepan, return to the boil, reduce the heat and keep the stock warm.

4 Meanwhile, heat the butter or oil in a large casserole dish or Dutch oven, add the flour and fry very slowly until the flour becomes a hazelnut colour, about 10 minutes: do not let the butter burn.

5 Add the garlic, onion and cayenne pepper and sauté for 2 minutes.

8 As the clams open (they will do so in stages), remove them to a plate with a slotted spoon. This will stop them overcooking. Add the okra to the pan.

9 Return the reserved chopped greens to the casserole and bring to the boil. Add a dash of Tabasco sauce.

10 Share the seafood, okra and greens between 4 large bowls, ladle the stock over the top, then serve with steamed white rice.

Shrimp Etouffée

6 tablespoons butter,
plus 2 tablespoons extra (see note)

4 tablespoons plain flour

1 large onion, chopped finely

1 green pepper, deseeded and diced

1 celery stalk, sliced

1 garlic clove, crushed

6 spring onions, coarsely sliced

¼ teaspoon cracked black pepper

¼ teaspoon cayenne pepper

a pinch of ground cumin

a large pinch of dried
chilli flakes, or to taste

300 ml fish stock (page 140)

1 tablespoon chopped fresh
flat leaf parsley

1 teaspoon lemon juice

1 kg peeled uncooked prawns (shrimp)

SERVES 4

The smell of butter and flour browning slowly in a large iron pot. The sizzle of freshly chopped onions, green peppers and spring onions added at just the right moment as the flour and butter turn a rich brown – all cooked in the dark roux. This is real, smoky-flavoured Cajun cooking. Often this dish is made with crawfish, which are plentiful in the waters of Louisiana, but I have made it with prawns (called 'shrimp' in America). Etouffée means 'smothered' – the dish is smothered by being covered with a lid, and the prawns cook gently in the steamy atmosphere.

Heat the butter in a heavy-based, flameproof casserole dish and mix in the flour. Stir it steadily for 3 minutes over a high heat so it first loses its moisture, then starts to take on a little colour. Immediately turn the heat to very low and continue stirring. Very gradually, both the flour and the butter will turn a rich chestnut-brown colour with a delicious biscuity flavour. This will take at least 12 minutes.

To stop the flour browning any further, stir in the onion, pepper, celery, garlic and half the spring onions. Cook at a medium heat until softened, then add the cracked pepper, cayenne, cumin, chilli flakes, stock and extra butter (see note below).

Bring to the boil, whisk until smooth, then taste and adjust the seasoning. Simmer for 15 minutes for the sauce to mature. Just before serving, add the remaining spring onions, parsley, lemon juice and finally the prawns. Bring to the boil, cover tightly with a lid or foil and cook very gently for 5 minutes, or until the prawns are opaque all the way through. The time will vary according to the size of the prawns. Do not overcook.

Serve over hot fluffy rice.

Note For best flavour, use shrimp butter instead of regular butter. You need prawn shells, so buy unpeeled prawns. Melt 125 g butter in a saucepan, add 125 ml water and the prawn shells and boil for 15 minutes. Strain and chill. The butter will form a hard layer on the surface, which can be removed and used in this and other seafood recipes.

A casserole from Chesapeake Bay where scallops and oysters are relatively cheap, though it could just as well come from anywhere on the East Coast, from Maine to South Carolina. The word 'casserole' in American cooking is often used to describe a dish of meats, fish and/or vegetables, bound by a rich sauce and topped with crumbled crackers or breadcrumbs, then browned in an oven or under a grill, as in this recipe.

3 ears of fresh corn
or 400 g frozen corn, thawed

100 g cooked rice

4 tablespoons butter

½ red pepper, deseeded
and diced

1 red chilli, finely sliced

3 spring onions, white and
green parts, sliced

about 12 scallops or
16–20 shucked fresh oysters,
with their liquor

1 teaspoon celery salt or salt

¼ teaspoon cracked black pepper

2 tablespoons fish stock
(page 140) or water

150 ml double cream

2–3 egg yolks, beaten

TOPPING

4 tablespoons butter

50 g fresh breadcrumbs

sweet paprika, for dusting

*4 heavy china teacups or ramekins,
or a 1 litre gratin dish, buttered*

SERVES 4

Fresh Corn and Scallop Casserole

If using fresh corn, cut the kernels off the cob with a sharp knife. Put the corn in a large saucepan of boiling salted water, blanch for 1 minute, then drain. Mix the corn with the cooked rice.

Melt the butter in a frying pan, add the diced pepper, chilli and spring onions and stir-fry for about 2 minutes until aromatic. Transfer to a plate.

Add the scallops or oysters to the pan and stir-fry for about 30 seconds to firm them a little. Season with salt and pepper, then divide them between the cups or ramekins. Spoon the corn-and-rice mixture over the top, then top with the reserved red pepper, chilli and spring onions.

Melt the butter for the topping in a small frying pan, add the breadcrumbs, then sauté for a few minutes until the crumbs are lightly golden.

Put the stock, cream and egg yolks in a bowl, together with any liquor from the oysters, if using, and beat lightly with a fork. Pour into the cups or ramekins.

Top with the breadcrumbs, sprinkle with paprika and cook in a preheated oven at 220°C (425°F) Gas 7 for 10 minutes. Brown the top under the grill if necessary, then serve.

This is a very simple recipe, so make the most of it with top quality free range chicken. The dumplings are cooked on top of the casserole so that they expand and stick together, forming a sort of lid on top. You can also cook them simply in a saucepan of boiling salted water.

Lemon Chicken with Dumplings

4 chicken breasts

2 cloves

1 bay leaf

10 peppercorns

2 celery stalks, sliced

½ onion, sliced

1 carrot, sliced

200 ml chicken stock (page 134)

MARINADE

shredded zest and juice of 1 lemon

½ teaspoon salt dissolved in 125 ml water

DUMPLING MIX

450 g plain flour

1 teaspoon salt

2 tablespoons baking powder

1 tablespoon chopped fresh flat leaf parsley (optional)

2 eggs, beaten

2 tablespoons butter, melted, plus 1 tablespoon extra, to glaze

4 tablespoons milk

SERVES 4

Mix the marinade ingredients in a shallow dish. Slice each chicken breast into 3 long strips, add to the dish, cover and chill for 4 hours or overnight.

Reserve the chicken breasts and transfer the marinating liquid to a flameproof casserole. Tie the cloves, bay leaf and peppercorns in a little muslin bag for easy removal later, then add to the casserole. Add the celery, onion, carrot and chicken stock. Bring to the boil on top of the stove, then reduce the heat and simmer for 20 minutes.

Meanwhile, to make the dumplings, sift the flour, salt and baking powder into a mixing bowl, then stir in the herbs, if using. Make a well in the centre of the flour, add the egg, the 2 tablespoons melted butter and milk, and stir with a wooden spoon until a soft ball forms. Do not overwork the mixture or the dumplings will become heavy when cooked. Divide the dough into 16 small balls and set aside. About 15 minutes before serving, drop the dumplings into a large saucepan of boiling salted water and return to the boil. Reduce the heat and simmer for 5 minutes. Carefully turn them over and continue simmering for a further 5 minutes. Using a slotted spoon, transfer them to a plate and glaze them with the remaining melted butter. Cover with clingfilm to prevent them drying out and keep them warm.

Remove the muslin bag from the casserole. Put the marinated chicken pieces into the casserole on top of the vegetables, then arrange the dumplings on top. Bring to the boil on top of the stove, then transfer to a preheated oven and cook at 200°C (400°F) Gas 6 for 20 minutes. Put under a preheated grill for about 3 minutes if you would like to brown the dumplings. Serve in the casserole.

A creamy, colourful dish with a beautiful aroma of herbs and fresh corn. It originates in New Orleans, where the Cajun word *maquechoux* means 'smothered in corn', which it certainly is! And what else would you serve with it other than a quick cornbread!

Chicken Maquechoux
with Cornbread

6 tablespoons corn or peanut oil

1 chicken, cut into serving pieces

½ teaspoon salt

2 onions, finely chopped

2 ears of fresh corn

1 green pepper, deseeded and finely chopped

2 tomatoes, skinned and deseeded

2 sprigs of thyme

125 ml single cream

1 tablespoon fresh basil, chopped

CORNBREAD

175 g yellow cornmeal

150 g plain flour

1 tablespoon sugar

4 teaspoons baking powder

1 teaspoon salt

a pinch of ground allspice

a pinch of ground white pepper

1 large egg

250 ml milk

65 ml vegetable shortening, plus 1½ tablespoons extra (or bacon fat), for greasing

SERVES 4

To make the cornbread, sift the dry ingredients into a mixing bowl. Add the egg, milk and the 65 ml shortening. Beat with a wooden spoon until smooth, about 1 minute.

Grease a 23 cm ovenproof frying pan with the remaining shortening or bacon fat, pour in the batter and bake in a preheated oven at 220°C (425°F) Gas 7 for 25 minutes until golden brown on top. Remove from the oven and cut into wedges.

To cook the chicken, heat 3 tablespoons of the oil in a non-stick frying pan, add the chicken pieces and fry until brown, turning them often and seasoning them with salt.

Heat the remaining oil in a heavy-based flameproof casserole, add the onion and 2 tablespoons water and cook until softened but not browned. (The water will help the onion cook without browning or using too much butter.)

Meanwhile, strip the corn from the cobs with a knife, cutting downwards from end to end and scraping any bits left behind. Add the corn to the casserole, then add the chopped peppers, tomatoes, thyme and a little more seasoning. Bring to the boil, then reduce to a simmer for 5 minutes to combine the flavours. Add the cream, bring to the boil and reduce a little of the liquid which the corn gives off.

Transfer the browned pieces of chicken to the casserole. Cook, uncovered, in a preheated oven at 190°C (375°F) Gas 5 until the chicken juices run clear when pricked with a fork, about 35 minutes. Stir in the basil and return the casserole to the oven for a further 5 minutes. Serve with the cornbread on the side.

Note For moist interior and crisp crust, you need a steamy oven atmosphere. Put a dish two-thirds filled with water on the floor of your oven before you begin to cook the cornbread. This clever trick works well with many home-baked breads.

2 ducks, about 1.5 kg each

40 g plain flour

500 ml chicken stock (page 134)

250 ml beef stock (page 136)

3 tablespoons redcurrant jelly

125 ml sweet sherry

125 ml sherry vinegar

1 tablespoon sugar

2 teaspoons crushed garlic

2 sprigs of fresh thyme

1 tablespoon chopped fresh
flat leaf parsley

sea salt and freshly
ground black pepper

SERVES 4

Cut each duck into 4, giving 8 pieces in all.

Heat a dry, non-stick frying pan. Working in batches if necessary, add the duck pieces, skin side down, and cook over a medium heat until well browned. Lots of the fat will run out, so pour it off into a bowl from time to time.

Set the breasts aside and put the legs in a flameproof casserole with a lid.

Pour off all but 3 tablespoons of the duck fat in the frying pan, add the flour and cook very slowly over a medium heat to a deep chestnut colour.

Add the stocks and bring to the boil, stirring all the time to make a smooth sauce. Add the jelly, sherry, sherry vinegar, sugar, garlic and herbs and continue stirring until the redcurrant jelly has dissolved.

Add a pinch of salt, then pour the mixture over the duck legs in the casserole. Bring to the boil on top of the stove, reduce to a simmer and cook for 1 hour. Add the duck breasts and continue cooking for a further 45 minutes.

Taste and adjust the seasoning, then serve.

Creole Duck

A typical Creole recipe with roux – deeply browned flour – plus the trinity of Creole flavourings; garlic, thyme and parsley. The sauce in which the duck cooks has a tantalizing, slightly sweet-sour overtone which cuts the richness of duck.

Yankee Pot Roast
with Braised Root Vegetables

The pot roast is one of the great American classics – and when it appears with braised vegetables, it becomes Yankee Pot Roast. You can also roast the vegetables instead of braising.

1 kg rolled silverside

3 tablespoons oil or bacon fat

1 tablespoon ground allspice

1 teaspoon salt

2 tablespoons plain flour

1 tablespoon dry mustard

150 ml red wine

500 ml beef stock (page 136)

6 tablespoons butter

4 parsnips, cut into 5 cm chunks

2 sweet potatoes, cut into 5 cm chunks

2 carrots, cut into 5 cm chunks

12 small red onions, cut into 4 wedges through the root

2 tablespoons cornflour

sea salt and freshly ground black pepper

SERVES 4

Put the silverside in a shallow dish. Put 1 tablespoon of the oil, allspice, salt, flour and mustard in a small bowl and mix to form a paste, adding more oil as necessary. Rub the silverside with the mixture, cover and marinate in the refrigerator for 3 hours or overnight.

Remove the meat and shake off any excess spices. Heat the remaining oil or bacon fat in a large frying pan, add the meat and brown on all sides. Transfer to an ovenproof casserole.

Add the wine to the frying pan, bring to the boil and cook until reduced by two-thirds. Add the stock and bring to the boil, pour over the meat, cover with a lid and cook in a preheated oven at 180°C (350°F) Gas 4 for 1½ hours or until tender.

Add the butter to the frying pan, heat gently, then add the vegetables and fry until they take on a little colour. Sprinkle with salt and pepper, cover with a lid and simmer in their own juices for 20 minutes. Keep them warm.

When the meat is cooked, drain off the liquid into a saucepan. Mix the cornflour with 3 tablespoons water and blend it into the liquid. Bring to the boil, then taste and adjust the seasoning. Pour the sauce back over the meat and vegetables and heat on top of the stove.

To serve, transfer the meat to a platter and arrange the reheated vegetables around. Serve the gravy separately.

Chili con Carne

This Texan classic is one of the most satisfying dishes of all and is justly world famous. Chili con Carne is almost always made with chilli powder, but I also like to make it with crushed dried chillies or sliced fresh ones. For timid tastebuds, adjust the quantity of chillies or chilli powder to suit.

Be sure to boil those beans well! Red kidney beans should be boiled hard for 15 minutes at the beginning of the cooking time. I then discard the water and cover them with fresh water before proceeding with the recipe.

Remember, don't salt dried beans until towards the end of cooking time, otherwise they will be tough and take at least twice as long to cook. You can, of course, use the canned variety, but use the liquid from the can in the gravy if you do – it's part of the thickening.

Like most beans, other than broad beans, red kidney beans are native to the Americas – to Mexico, in fact. Smoky and delicious in flavour, their more elegant cousins are the white cannellini and the infant green flageolets.

Chili con Carne
step-by-step

500 g dried red kidney beans, washed

½ teaspoon salt

2 tablespoons shortening, corn oil or beef dripping

2 onions, sliced

3 garlic cloves, sliced

1 kg braising steak, cut into 1.5 cm cubes

2 tablespoons plain flour

2 tablespoons tomato paste

¼–½ tablespoon chilli powder, dried chilli flakes, or 1–4 whole red serrano chillies, deseeded if preferred, then chopped

1 green pepper, halved, deseeded and chopped

¼ teaspoon ground cumin

1 litre beef stock

sea salt, to taste

TO SERVE

a little chopped coriander

sour cream (optional)

flour tortillas, warmed, or crackers

SERVES 4–6

1 Put the beans in a bowl, cover with cold water and let soak for at least 3 hours or overnight.* When ready to cook, drain, then rinse in cold water.

*If short of time, put them in a saucepan, cover with cold water, bring to the boil, simmer for 2 minutes, remove from the heat, cover and let soak for 1 hour. Drain.

2 Put the beans in a saucepan, cover with cold water, bring to the boil and boil hard for 15 minutes to remove the toxins. Drain, cover with fresh water and return to the boil. Simmer for 1–4 hours or until tender (the time depends on the age of the beans): top up with boiling water as necessary. Add ½ teaspoon salt 15 minutes before the end of cooking. Set aside.

3 Put the shortening, oil or dripping in a large frying pan and heat until melted. Add the onion and garlic and cook gently until softened and lightly browned, about 15 minutes. Transfer to a plate and keep them warm.

4 Add the steak cubes to the pan, in batches if necessary – do not crowd the pan. Fry until browned on all sides.

5 Stir in the flour and mix well.

6 Add the tomato paste, chilli powder or flakes or fresh chillies, green pepper, cumin and stock and strain in any cooking liquid from the cooked beans or the liquid from the can, if using canned beans. Bring to the boil, transfer to a casserole or saucepan and simmer on top of the stove or in a preheated oven at 150°C (300°F) Gas 2 for 1¼ hours, or until the meat is tender.

7 Remove from the oven, season to taste, stir in the beans, return to the oven and cook for a further 30 minutes.

8 Sprinkle with chopped coriander and serve with a spoonful of sour cream, if using, and warmed tortillas or crackers.

Brunswick Stew

Taking its name from Brunswick County in Virginia, this is a dish designed for a large number of hungry people: it's not sophisticated, just full of goodness. The main ingredients are chicken, ham and shin of beef cut in the same way as osso buco, which could be used instead. (I was fascinated to discover that squirrel used to be one of the ingredients – now that's something that would scare some people!) Traditionally, the stew was thickened with mashed potatoes, but, in this modern version, they are served separately.

1 kg chicken, cut in 4, or 4 leg portions

1 ham bone or uncooked smoked gammon

750 g shin bone beef or osso buco

1 bay leaf

1.75 litres ham stock or water

1 onion, sliced

500 g tomatoes, halved, deseeded and chopped

250 g celery, chopped

250 g green lima (butter beans) or broad beans

1½ tablespoons chopped fresh basil

1½ tablespoons chopped fresh flat leaf parsley

1 ear of fresh corn (optional)

1 red serrano chilli, deseeded and sliced

1 teaspoon cracked black pepper

sea salt

buttery mashed potatoes, to serve

SERVES 8–10

Put the chicken, ham bone or gammon, beef and bay leaf into a large stockpot or casserole and cover with the stock or water. Do not season unless the gammon is unsalted. Cover with a lid, bring to the boil, then reduce the heat and simmer for about 40 minutes.

Lift out the chicken pieces and ham bone or gammon and transfer to a large plate. Let cool and then cut off their meat in chunks and set aside. Discard the bones.

Continue simmering until the beef comes away from the centre bone, about 2–4 hours. Discard the bone and add the beef to the chicken and gammon.

If necessary, reduce the pan juices to about 850 ml by boiling hard, then add the onions, tomatoes, celery, lima or broad beans, basil and parsley. Cover and simmer for about 20 minutes until done.

Return the meats to the casserole. If using corn, strip the kernels from the cob and add them to the casserole. Add the chilli and pepper, simmer for 5 minutes, taste and adjust the seasoning. Serve with piles of mashed potatoes.

Vegetarian Green Chili
with Hominy Cakes

4 tablespoons sunflower oil

2 onions, finely chopped

1–2 fresh red chillies

2 garlic cloves, crushed

1 teaspoon chopped fresh oregano

1 teaspoon ground cumin

1 teaspoon Tabasco sauce

1 teaspoon sweet paprika

a pinch of cayenne pepper

200 g canned chopped tomatoes

½ teaspoon salt

500 g spring cabbage greens

500 g spinach, well rinsed

250 g green beans

1 cucumber, peeled and cubed

HOMINY CAKES

625 ml cooked fine hominy grits, by measure

2 tablespoons plain flour, plus extra for coating

1 egg

1 teaspoon sweet paprika

1 egg, beaten

4 tablespoons chopped fresh flat leaf parsley

2 tablespoons butter

2 tablespoons peanut oil

sea salt and freshly ground black pepper

SERVES 4

Hominy is a kind of cornmeal – cook it according to the directions on the packet. If you prefer, you can make these cakes using cooked polenta instead, which is another ground corn product. Both make an excellent base for a fiery sauce like this.

To make the Chili, heat the oil in a frying pan, add the onions, chillies and garlic and fry until softened. Add the oregano and cumin and cook for 2 minutes, then add the Tabasco, paprika, cayenne, tomatoes and salt. Simmer for 5 minutes.

Bring a large saucepan of salted water to the boil, add the greens and cook for about 10 minutes, adding the spinach for the last 2 minutes, just until wilted. Remove all the greens from the water, drain and squeeze dry. Arrange in a large oval baking dish. Blanch the beans and cucumber in the same boiling water for 2 minutes, then drain and distribute evenly over the greens.

Pour the sauce over the greens and simmer in a preheated oven 200°C (400°F) Gas 6 for 20 minutes.

To make the Hominy Cakes, put the cooked grits in a bowl, stir in the flour, egg, paprika, salt and pepper. Make hamburger-sized patties from the mixture, patting them between your palms. Dip the cakes first in beaten egg, then in the chopped parsley, then in flour. Heat the butter and oil in a wide frying pan. Add the hominy cakes and fry on both sides until golden brown. Serve on heated plates with the chili greens on top.

Caribbean Vegetable Stew

'Spicy mixtures of island vegetables, bound with tomatoes and red hot chillies' – a perfect description of many vegetable dishes in the Caribbean. In Jamaica, callaloo leaves would be used instead of spinach – and the root of the same plant is a yam known as dasheen. I've used sweet potato as a substitute. A plantain is a large cooking banana (some have delightful pale pink flesh), but you can use ordinary green bananas instead.

Put the oil in a large, flameproof casserole, add the onion and cook until softened and translucent. Add the allspice, cumin, nutmeg, chillies, garlic, ginger, tomatoes and parsley and cook to a sauce. Season with the soy sauce. Add the sweet potato, red onions and plantains or bananas, cover and simmer for 20 minutes, then add the carrots and spinach and cook for a further 5 minutes, adding the mangetout for the last 2 minutes. Season, scatter with chives, then serve.

4 tablespoons sunflower oil

1 onion, chopped

2 teaspoon ground allspice

1 teaspoon ground cumin

¼ teaspoon freshly grated nutmeg

4 fresh red chillies, deseeded and chopped

4 garlic cloves, crushed

5 cm fresh ginger, peeled and grated

5 tomatoes, skinned, deseeded and diced

1 tablespoon chopped fresh flat leaf parsley

2 tablespoons soy sauce

1 sweet potato, peeled and cubed

2 red onions, quartered

2 plantains or green bananas, peeled and cut into chunks

6 baby carrots, trimmed

500 g baby spinach, rinsed

50 g mangetout

freshly ground black pepper

snipped fresh chives, to serve

SERVES 4

Europe has more variations of the casserole than anywhere else. Ragout or *pot au feu*, navarin or hotpot, tian or *pochoise* – all are forms of casserole, often given the name of the vessel in which they are cooked.

Some, like the Steak and Kidney Pudding, are cooked in an 'all-in-one' method with no preliminary browning of the ingredients. Others, like *Coq au Vin*, need more sophisticated treatment: the bird is browned in butter and the dark gravy enriched with reduced red wine.

At one time, a stock was kept simmering in a large cauldron over an open fire. A pot containing all the necessary casserole ingredients was suspended inside the cauldron, surrounded by the liquid, and the stew was 'jugged'. This method of very slow cooking is replicated both in the French bain-marie system and the modern slow cooker, where the temperature is kept significantly below boiling point, but high enough to cook protein.

Many of these recipes were originally cooked over an open fire of peat or wood. Later on, when people still did not have ovens in their own houses, but village bakeries did, long, slow cooking was done after the bread had been made, often on a falling temperature and making use of all the latent heat left in a solid fuel oven.

Closed ovens in kitchen ranges have come on the scene only in the past two hundred years or so, but have revolutionized casserole cooking everywhere.

But Europe, to my mind, is still the casserole capital of the world. Her people, intrepid travellers all – and determined colonizers – have taken with them the dishes of their homelands to every continent, from the Americas to Africa, from India to the Antipodes.

EUROPE

A creamy, garlicky, fish stew that's a meal on its own. It is quite different from its sister soup, the bouillabaisse: it is made without tomato, but instead with a rich liaison of egg yolks and mayonnaise beaten in at the end. Traditionally, it would include sea bass, John Dory, whiting, monkfish, sea bream, red gurnard, conger eel and whatever was fresh and firm on the day.

La Bourride

1 tablespoon olive oil

1 onion, sliced

1 fennel bulb, sliced

3 garlic cloves, sliced

peeled zest of ½ orange

1 fresh bouquet garni (sprigs of parsley, thyme, bay leaf and celery, tied up with kitchen string)

250 ml white wine

1.5 litres fish stock (page 140)

at least 1.5 kg white fish, cut into large pieces (see recipe introduction)

4 egg yolks

1 garlic clove, crushed

100 ml olive oil

sea salt and freshly ground black pepper

TO SERVE

boiled potatoes or triangles of white bread, toasted

SERVES 4

Heat the oil in a large, flameproof casserole, add the onion, fennel, garlic, orange zest and bouquet garni and fry for 5 minutes without browning.

Add the wine, then bring to the boil until reduced to about 2–3 tablespoons. Add the stock, bring to the boil, then season with salt and plenty of pepper.

Carefully add the pieces of fish, cover with a lid, transfer to a preheated oven and cook at 180°C (350°F) Gas 4 for about 20–25 minutes. Remove from the oven and carefully drain the liquid into a large saucepan. Keep the fish warm in the casserole, but remove the bouquet garni.

Taste the liquid and, if the flavour isn't strong enough, bring to the boil and simmer until reduced to about 850 ml.

Put the egg yolks and garlic into a small food processor or bowl, then gradually work in the olive oil, drop by drop, to form a thick mayonnaise. Gradually whisk the mixture into the fish stock. Still stirring, bring the mixture almost to the boil (do not let it boil, or the eggs will scramble).

Remove from the heat, then strain the sauce back over the fish in the casserole. Serve with boiled potatoes or the traditional accompaniment of crisp toast.

There may seem a lot of mustard in this sauce, but, when you cook mustard, it loses its heat and you are left with a delicious flavour which no one can quite place once the poaching liquid has been added.

Traditional Fish Pie

500 ml milk

750 g smoked or fresh haddock, skinned

275 g unsalted butter

1 tablespoon dry English mustard powder

4 tablespoons plain flour

2 hard-boiled eggs, peeled and quartered

1 kg floury potatoes

sea salt and freshly ground black pepper

SERVES 4

Put the milk in a wide saucepan, heat just to boiling point, then add the fish. Turn off the heat and let poach until opaque – do not overcook.

Meanwhile, melt 125 g of the butter in another saucepan, then stir in the mustard and flour. Remove from the heat and strain the poaching liquid into the pan.

Arrange the fish and eggs in a shallow pie dish or casserole.

Return the pan to the heat and, whisking vigorously to smooth out any lumps, bring the mixture to the boil. Season with salt and pepper if necessary. (Take care: if you are using smoked fish, it may be salty enough.) Pour the sauce into the casserole and mix carefully with the fish and eggs.

Cook the potatoes in boiling salted water until soft, then drain. Return to the pan. Melt the remaining 150 g butter in a small saucepan. Reserve 4 tablespoons of this butter and stir the remainder into the potatoes. Mash well and season with salt and pepper. Spoon the mixture carefully over the sauced fish, brush generously with the reserved butter and transfer to a preheated oven at 200°C (400°F) Gas 6 for 20 minutes, or until nicely browned.

Note If no smoked haddock is available, add 125 g smoked salmon, finely sliced, sprinkled over the poached fish just before adding the sauce.

France's most famous stew is *Coq au Vin* (chicken in wine). To be authentic, it should contain mushrooms, bacon lardons and caramelized baby onions. In the old days, when *coqs* were old cocks, the bird was simmered in red wine for hours, like a daube. Now it is nearly impossible to get an old bird, so modern recipes use a young bird and a shorter cooking time.

Coq au Vin

1 large chicken, preferably free range or corn-fed, cut into serving pieces

leaves from 1 sprig of thyme, finely chopped

50 g butter

60 ml brandy

1 bottle rich red wine, 750 ml

750 ml chicken stock (page 134)

4 tomatoes, skinned and deseeded, or 2 teaspoons tomato paste

2 garlic cloves, crushed

1 bay leaf

sea salt and freshly ground black pepper

ROUX

50 g butter

2 tablespoons plain flour

TO SERVE

125 g smoked bacon, in the piece, cut into lardons

125 g butter

125 g button mushrooms, sliced

12 baby onions

SERVES 4

Season the chicken pieces with salt and pepper and sprinkle with the thyme leaves. Put the butter into a large, flameproof casserole and heat until it begins to brown. Add the chicken to the casserole and sauté, skin side down, until golden brown.

Remove the casserole from the heat, pour over the brandy and set it alight if you wish – otherwise let it boil away so the alcohol evaporates. Using tongs or a slotted spoon, remove the chicken to a plate and keep it warm.

Pour the wine into the casserole, bring to the boil and reduce to about 3–4 tablespoons. Add the tomatoes or paste, garlic and bay leaf and mix well.

To make the roux, heat the butter in a small frying pan, add the flour and cook, stirring, until the mixture is a pale brown. Stir it into the mixture in the casserole.

Reserve 250 ml of the stock, stir the remainder into the casserole and bring to the boil. Add the chicken and any juices that have run onto the plate. Season to taste, cover with a lid and cook in a preheated oven at 180°C (350°F) Gas 4 for 40 minutes, or until the chicken juices run clear when pricked with a fork.

Meanwhile, bring a saucepan of water to the boil, add the bacon, boil for 1 minute, then drain. Add the bacon into the casserole halfway through the cooking time.

Put 75 g of the serving butter in a small frying pan, add the mushrooms and sauté for 5 minutes. Transfer to the casserole for the last 5 minutes of cooking time.

Add the remaining butter to the frying pan, add the onions and sauté until browned, about 5 minutes. Add the reserved 250 ml chicken stock, bring to the boil and simmer until tender and the stock has been absorbed, about 10 minutes.

Serve on heated dinner plates, topping each serving a share of the mushrooms, bacon and golden onions.

Avgolémono – the liaison of egg yolks and lemon juice stirred into a dish before serving – is one of the hallmarks of Greek cooking. It produces a creamy texture without the heaviness of cream, as well as a refreshing effect which counteracts any richness.

Creamy Greek Lemon Chicken

50 g butter

2 tablespoons olive oil

1.5 kg chicken, cut into serving pieces, or 1.5 kg chicken pieces

1 onion, sliced

1 carrot, sliced

1 small celery stalk or slice of fennel, cut into chunks

600 ml chicken stock (page 134)

1 tablespoon cornflour

2 egg yolks

2 tablespoons fresh lemon juice

sea salt and freshly ground black pepper

TO SERVE

zest of 1 lemon, cut into fine strips or removed with a zester

sprigs of dill or 1 tablespoon chopped fresh dill

SERVES 4

Heat the butter and oil in a large, flameproof casserole. Season the chicken pieces, onion, carrot and celery or fennel, add them to the casserole and sauté gently without browning, but turning them over from time to time, about 15 minutes.

Add the stock, bring to the boil, then season to taste. Cover and transfer to a preheated oven at 170°C (350°F) Gas 4 for 40 minutes, or until the chicken is cooked (the juices should run clear when pricked through the thickest part with a fork or skewer).

Put the cornflour into a small cup or bowl, add 4 tablespoons water and stir until loose. (This is called slaking.)

Remove the casserole from the heat, pour off the liquid into another saucepan, bring to the boil and reduce to about 300 ml. Remove from the heat and let cool for 5 minutes. Put the egg yolks in a bowl, beat well, then whisk in 1 tablespoon of the lemon juice. Whisk the mixture into the sauce, a little at a time, and very slowly. Taste and adjust the seasoning. Add the remaining tablespoon of lemon juice if it needs a little more acidity. Reserve a tablespoon or so of the lemon zest and stir the remainder into the sauce.

Remove the chicken from the oven and pour the sauce over. Serve topped with chopped dill and the reserved lemon zest.

Butter is the frying medium in the area of Italy with which this recipe is associated. It is traditionally served with *Risotto alla Milanese* – a most delicious concoction of saffron, arborio rice, white wine, chicken stock and butter. Unquestionably, resist the temptation to cook this dish in olive oil.

Osso Buco

125 g butter

1 onion, chopped

1 carrot, chopped

2 celery stalks, chopped

3 garlic cloves, sliced

300 g canned Italian tomatoes

leaves from 2 sprigs of thyme

2 tablespoons chopped fresh flat leaf parsley

2 bay leaves

125 ml peanut or sunflower oil

100 g plain flour, seasoned with salt and pepper

4 large slices veal shanks, about 5–7 cm thick, 300 g each

250 ml white wine

500 ml chicken stock (page 134)

sea salt and freshly ground black pepper

SERVES 4

Heat the butter in a large frying pan, add the onion, carrot, celery and garlic and cook gently until softened and translucent – take care not to burn the butter. Add the tomatoes and herbs and simmer for 10 minutes to make a sauce. Transfer to a casserole and set aside. Add the oil to the frying pan and heat gently.

Put the flour, salt and pepper in a plastic bag, add the veal and shake to coat. Add to the frying pan and sauté until browned on all sides. Transfer to the casserole.

To deglaze the frying pan, add the wine, bring to the boil and reduce to 2 tablespoons. Add the stock and scrape up any sediment from the base of the pan, so as not to lose any flavour. Bring to the boil, season with salt and pepper, then transfer to the casserole. The liquid should nearly cover the meat: if not, top up with boiling water.

Cover tightly with a lid and cook in a preheated oven at 170°C (325°F) Gas 3 for about 1½ hours, checking the liquid from time to time to see that the meat is not drying out. When the meat is tender, lift it onto a serving dish and check that the sauce is of a coating consistency. If it is too thin, transfer to the top of the stove and simmer until reduced. There should be about 750 ml. Pour it over the meat and serve with *Risotto alla Milanese* or mashed potatoes.

Risotto alla Milanese Put a large pinch of saffron threads into a bowl, pour over 125 ml boiling water and let soak for 30 minutes. Put 1 litre rich chicken stock in a saucepan, bring to the boil and add the saffron and its soaking liquid. Melt 100 g butter in a large saucepan, add 1 finely chopped onion and sauté very gently for 5 minutes until softened but not browned. Add 500 g superfino arborio risotto rice and sauté gently until it whitens, about 5 minutes. Add 250 ml dry white wine and let it bubble away to about 1 teaspoon. Add a ladle of the stock and simmer until absorbed. Continue adding stock, a ladle at a time, until all the stock has been used and the rice is still al dente. Stir in 200 g grated Parmesan cheese and serve with the Osso Buco.

Daubes are dishes in which the meat is sealed in a lidded casserole and simmered in wine for a long time and is so soft that it can be cut with a spoon. The wine used here is a white one, which is rather unexpected with beef. It gives a more acid pungency to the dish and goes well with olives.

Provençal Daube of Beef

2 tablespoons olive oil

500 g onions, sliced

1 kg rolled rib of beef, in the piece

2 garlic cloves, sliced

2 tomatoes, chopped

1 carrot, sliced crossways

2 sprigs of thyme

2 fresh bay leaves

150 ml white wine

6 green olives, pitted

6 black olives, pitted

sea salt and freshly ground black pepper

SERVES 4

Heat the oil in a large frying pan, add the onions and sauté until softened but not browned. Transfer to a casserole just big enough to hold the beef.

Add the rolled rib of beef to the frying pan, brown it on all sides, then transfer to the casserole.

Add the garlic, tomatoes, carrot, thyme and bay leaves to the frying pan and mix well. Sauté until lightly browned, then pack the mixture around the beef in the casserole.

Pour the wine into the frying pan, scraping any brown bits into the liquid. Season with salt and pepper and pour the mixture over the beef. Cover with a lid, transfer to a preheated oven at 150°C (300°F) Gas 2 and cook for 3 hours until all the liquid has been absorbed. If necessary, take the lid off for the last 40 minutes to reduce the excess liquid.

Add the olives to the casserole, heat through for 5 minutes, then serve with lots of creamy mashed potatoes and a few steamed baby carrots – the beef should by now be so tender that it falls to pieces when touched.

Irish Carbonnade

Carbonnades are native to Belgium and northern France, where they are always flavoured with beer. I find good Irish stout much superior. A carbonnade uses caramelized sugar to sweeten the gravy. In this version, stout gives an extra touch of bitterness and this must be corrected to be pleasing. Lots of sweet shallots or pickling onions will also add to the sweetness.

2 tablespoons duck or goose fat, or peanut or sunflower oil

750 g skirt steak or casserole beef, cut into 3 cm cubes

3 tablespoons sugar

1 onion, chopped

2 tablespoons plain flour

12 shallots

500 ml hot beef stock (page 136)

375 ml stout, such as Guinness

2 tablespoons red wine vinegar

3 cloves

2 bay leaves

sea salt and freshly ground black pepper

SERVES 4

Heat the fat or oil in a large frying pan. Season the meat with salt and pepper, add to the pan and sauté until browned on all sides. Transfer to a large, flameproof casserole.

Add the sugar to the frying pan and let it cook until it becomes a good chestnut colour. Add the onion, flour and shallots and mix well for about 30 seconds. Stir in the stock and stout. Bring to the boil and cook for 1 minute. Add the vinegar, cloves, bay leaves and a little more seasoning, then pour it all over the meat in the casserole. Mix well.

Cover the casserole and let simmer very gently on top of the stove or in a preheated oven at 170°C (325°F), Gas 3 for 1½–2 hours. Remove from the heat or the oven and pour off the liquid into a separate saucepan or frying pan. Bring to the boil and simmer to reduce the liquid to a coating consistency. Return it to the casserole and serve. Piles of creamy mashed potatoes and sautéed mushrooms would be suitable accompaniments.

Steak and Kidney Pudding

The richness of the gravy in a steak and kidney pudding is unique. It is produced by the meats giving all their juices to thicken and flavour the stock in the pudding without the liquid having come to the boil. Once the pudding has been broached, the gravy actually thickens even more and should be thinned down with more stock unless you like a very thick gravy. I know of no other dish that works like this, certainly not a steak and kidney pie. It is a very interesting example of casserole cooking and is classic British food at its best. Serve the pudding wrapped in a linen napkin, with a small jug of extra stock for thinning down the gravy.

Steak and Kidney Pudding
step-by-step

500 g beef kidney

4 tablespoons plain flour

1 teaspoon salt

¼ teaspoon freshly ground black pepper

750 g shin or chuck steak, cut into 3 cm cubes*

2 onions, chopped

1 garlic clove, crushed (optional)

600 ml beef stock (page 134) or water

SUET CRUST

500 g self-raising flour

1 teaspoon salt

250 g suet or shortening

1 pudding basin, 2.25 litre (4 pint) capacity

SERVES 4–6

*The cooking time will differ for different kinds of meat. In Step 10, chuck will take 4 hours, while shin will take 6 hours.

1 To make the suet crust, put the flour, salt and suet into a bowl, add about 600 ml water, or enough to make a firm mixture. Mix to form a ball.

Reserve one-third of the dough to make the lid and transfer the remainder to a floured surface. Roll out to a disc 40 cm in diameter.

2 Cut out a wedge from the disc – this will allow it to fit the pudding basin easily. Use to line the basin, letting it overlap the edges by 2 cm all round (trim back any excess). Stick any joins together with a little water.

6 Heat the stock, season to taste, then pour about half the stock over the meat to cover it. Reserve the remaining stock.

Roll out the remaining dough to make a disc just big enough to cover the top of the basin.

7 Fold the overlapping edges of the pastry inwards over the top of the meat and brush the top edge with water.

3 Cut the kidney into 2 cm chunks, discarding all the membrane. You will lose about a quarter of the weight.

4 Put the flour, salt and pepper into a plastic bag, seal and shake. Add the steak and kidney and, holding the neck of the bag tightly, shake it vigorously until all the meat is evenly coated with the seasoned flour.

5 Shake off any excess flour and transfer all the meat into the basin. Sprinkle with the onion and garlic, if using, as you do so.

8 Put the lid of pastry on top of the basin and crimp the edges inside the rim to seal the pudding. Don't worry if a little stock escapes: it will be absorbed.

9 Fold a large sheet of foil to make a pleat down the middle to allow for expansion. Put on top of the basin and tie a length of kitchen string firmly around the edge, under the lip of the basin. Tie a 'handle' of kitchen string from side to side, to make the pudding easier to lift in and out of the pan.

10 Lower into a casserole or large saucepan, three-quarters fill the pan with boiling water and cover with a lid. Return to the boil, reduce the heat and let simmer for 4–6 hours, topping it up with boiling water from time to time.

Serve. After the first helping has been served, gently mix in the rest of the stock to thin the gravy for second helpings.

Serve a navarin when the new season's vegetables are being harvested and the lamb is just that little bit older. To give the gravy that rich colour and sweet flavour, a little sugar is sprinkled either onto the lamb as it is browned, or into the pan, which makes it easier to control. It is then caramelized: the darker the sugar becomes, the less sweet the stew will be.

Navarin of Lamb

1 kg boneless shoulder of lamb

1 tablespoon butter

1 tablespoon sugar

2 tablespoons plain flour

600 ml lamb or beef stock (page 136)

4 tomatoes, skinned and deseeded, or 200 g canned Italian plum tomatoes

2 garlic cloves, crushed

1 teaspoon chopped fresh thyme leaves

1 sprig of rosemary

1 bay leaf

sea salt and freshly ground black pepper

SPRING VEGETABLES

8 new potatoes, scraped and cooked

8 baby carrots, scraped and cooked

8 baby white turnips, cooked

125 g green peas, cooked

125 g green beans, cooked and cut into 1 cm strips

SERVES 4

Cut the lamb into 2 cm cubes, discarding any fat. Heat the butter in a heavy frying pan. Season the lamb and sauté in 2 batches, browning the pieces evenly all over and draining them of fat as they are put aside onto a dish.

Reserve 3 tablespoons of the fat in the pan and discard the rest. Sprinkle the sugar into the pan and let caramelize to a deep golden brown. (Take care not to caramelize it too much – it burns easily.) Quickly mix in the flour, then return the meat to the pan and mix well: this will let the flour cook a little.

Add the stock, then the tomatoes, garlic and herbs. Stir gently and bring to the boil. Season to taste, then transfer to a lidded casserole, cover and simmer in a preheated oven at 190°C (375°F) Gas 5 for 40–50 minutes or until the meat is tender.

If there is too much liquid, strain it off into a saucepan, bring to the boil and simmer until reduced to about 600 ml. Taste and adjust the seasoning, then add the cooked vegetables. Mix them gently through the liquid, then transfer them and the liquid to the casserole, stir gently, then reheat in the oven for about 10 minutes. Serve.

This is a very simple dish but surprisingly effective considering how few ingredients there are, so make sure you adjust the seasoning carefully as it makes such a difference. Ideally, each steak should be about 2 cm thick and weigh about 250 g. Trim the stem end only of the okra, taking off the tiniest layer of the already-cut surface, to discourage the sticky liquid from oozing out.

Greek Braised Lamb with Okra

3 tablespoons olive oil

4 lamb steaks, about 1 kg, cut from the leg and deboned

1 small onion, sliced

2 garlic cloves, crushed

4 tomatoes, skinned and deseeded

250 g okra, trimmed

sea salt and freshly ground black pepper

TO SERVE

new potatoes

chopped fresh flat leaf parsley

SERVES 4

Heat the oil in a large, wide, shallow, flameproof casserole or saucepan. Season the meat with salt and pepper, add to the pan and brown the pieces all over. Remove the meat with a slotted spoon, put on a plate and set aside in a warm place.

Add the onion and garlic to the pan and cook until softened and lightly browned. Add the tomatoes and simmer to a pulp.

Return the lamb to the pan, turn to coat, taste and adjust the seasoning and cover with a lid. Bring to the boil on top of the stove, then transfer to a preheated oven and simmer at 180°C (350°F) Gas 4 for 20 minutes.

Add the okra, cover and simmer for a further 20 minutes, removing the lid for the last 10 minutes of cooking time, to let the liquid reduce enough to just coat the meat without becoming oily. Serve with new potatoes and sprinkle with chopped parsley.

A 'hand' of pork is part of the shoulder of the animal. It is much the best part, to my mind, for roasting or braising, as it has just the right amount of fat, whereas the leg is so lean as to make it difficult to keep moist. Anyway, a certain amount of fat is needed in this dish to moisten the beans – or perhaps it's the other way round and the beans are needed to mop up the juices. Either way, it makes for a scrumptious dinner.

Tuscan Pork and Bean Casserole

250 g dried cannellini beans
4 tablespoons olive oil
350 g carrots, cut into 3 cm chunks
4 onions, peeled but left whole
4 small turnips
1 sprig of thyme
1 bay leaf
6 peppercorns
6 garlic cloves, or to taste
2 kg hand of pork
250 g rindless smoked streaky bacon in the piece, cut into chunks
750 g small potatoes, peeled
250 g fresh green beans
sea salt and freshly ground black pepper

SERVES 4

Put the dried beans in a bowl, cover with water and let soak overnight. Drain, transfer the beans to a saucepan, cover with water again and bring to the boil. Drain and discard this water, reserving the beans to add to the stew.

Heat the oil in a large ovenproof casserole with a lid, then stir in the carrots, onions, turnips, thyme, bay leaf, peppercorns and garlic. Sauté gently until softened but not browned.

Meanwhile, cut the rind off the pork and reserve it. Add the pork, its rind, the bacon chunks and the drained beans to the casserole. Cover with water, add salt and pepper and bring to the boil on top of the stove. Transfer to a preheated oven and simmer at 170°C (325°F) Gas 3 for 1½ hours, or until the beans are tender.

After 1 hour, taste and adjust the seasoning, then add the potatoes for the last 30 minutes and the fresh green beans for the last 5 minutes.

To serve, remove and discard the pork rind, lift the meat onto a dish and carve into thick slices. Add the vegetables and beans to the dish and serve with a separate small jug of the cooking juices.

Try a *choucroute* at least once in your life and you'll be hooked. It reheats very well and doesn't mind waiting, so cook more than you need and have it twice. Jazz it up with duck confit or roast goose for a special treat (home-cooked or from a French deli). Goose or duck fat is also sold by the jar in the same delis and adds considerably to the flavour. Butter is also good, but just don't use olive oil – it's completely the wrong flavour, from the wrong part of the world.

Choucroute Garnie

1 kg bottled sauerkraut, 1 litre by volume

5 tablespoons goose fat or butter

250 g streaky bacon pieces

1 carrot, sliced

1 onion, sliced

1 bay leaf

2 sprigs of thyme

6 peppercorns

125 ml white wine

500 ml chicken stock

4 pork neck cutlets

8 frankfurters

sea salt and freshly ground black pepper

SERVES 4

Drain the sauerkraut, empty it into a large saucepan and cover with water. Stir well, empty into a colander, then drain.

Heat 3 tablespoons of the the goose fat or butter in a large, flameproof casserole, add the bacon, carrot, onion, herbs and peppercorns and cook gently for 5 minutes. Add the wine, bring to the boil and reduce by half.

Add the stock and stir in the drained sauerkraut. Cover with a lid, bring to the boil and cook in a preheated oven at 170°C (325°F) Gas 3 for 2 hours.

Meanwhile, heat the remaining goose fat or butter in a frying pan, add the pork cutlets, season with salt and pepper and sauté until browned. Tuck the pork cutlets into the sauerkraut for the last hour. Add the frankfurters for the final 5 minutes.

Note Choucroute is traditionally served on a large platter in the middle of the table. Since Alsace is its original home, a cold beer or a glass of spicy gewürztraminer would be a suitable accompaniment.

Cassoulet de Toulouse

Cassoulets, the pride of many southern areas in France, are named after the region from which they come, *Cassoulet de Toulouse* being one of the most famous. They show off the local garlic sausages, while the beans also play an important part – some flageolets are the pale green variety, not very often found fresh outside the area. Luckily, all this doesn't affect the magnificence of the dish, which calls out for robust red wine and genial company. Don't worry if the dish has to wait. Just add a bit more hot stock or water to the pot and lower the oven temperature until ready to serve.

Cassoulet de Toulouse
step-by-step

500 g dried flageolet beans

250 g smoked gammon, uncooked

about 8 tablespoons butter, olive oil or goose fat

500 g boneless shoulder of lamb, cubed

500 g rindless belly of pork, cubed

4 garlic cloves, crushed

2 tomatoes, skinned and chopped

2 sprigs of thyme

2 sprigs of marjoram, or ½ teaspoon dried

600 ml beef stock (page 136)

200 g whole piece of garlic sausage, cut into bite-sized pieces

4 tablespoons fresh breadcrumbs

sea salt and freshly ground black pepper

SERVES 6

1 Put the beans in a bowl, cover with cold water and let soak for at least 8 hours, but preferably overnight. Next day, drain them, put in a large, flameproof casserole, cover with fresh water, bring to the boil on top of the stove, then drain again. Cover with cold water for a third time.

2 Add the gammon, bring to the boil, reduce the heat and simmer for about 45 minutes, being careful not to let the beans start to disintegrate.

6 Strain the beans into a bowl, reserving their liquid. Spread some of the beans in a thick layer in the bottom of a deep casserole.

7 Add a layer of meat, another layer of sausage and a layer of beans. Repeat until all have been used up, finishing with a layer of beans.

3 Meanwhile, heat 2 tablespoons of the butter, oil or goose fat in a large frying pan, add the lamb and pork pieces in batches and fry until lightly brown, adding extra butter, oil or fat as necessary. Do not crowd the pan and remove the meat to a plate between batches. (They are cooked in batches so that they fry, rather than boiling in their own juices.)

4 Return all the meat to the pan, add the garlic, tomatoes, herbs, salt and pepper. Cook for 1–2 minutes, or until the tomatoes soften to a purée.

Add enough beef stock to cover, bring to the boil and simmer for 40 minutes, or until the meat is tender and the gravy is well reduced and concentrated.

5 Remove the gammon from the beans, transfer to a cutting board and cut into bite-sized pieces.

8 Add the meat cooking liquid, then the reserved bean liquid, filling the casserole almost to the top.

9 Heat 3 tablespoons of the butter, olive oil or goose fat in a frying pan, add the breadcrumbs and fry until golden brown. Remove from the heat, then drain.

10 Sprinkle the crumbs over the top of the cassoulet, then cook in a preheated oven at 180°C (350°F) Gas 4 for about 1½ hours until crusty. Serve with a green salad and plenty of red wine.

A traditional hotpot was an earthenware vessel with a tight-fitting lid, tall enough to take mutton cutlets standing upright, so it was very tall! Nowadays, any casserole will do, as the name refers to the contents rather than the pot. The Lancashire version is always topped with a lid of sliced or chunked potatoes and usually contains beef as well as lamb. This recipe is just one of several local variations; other hotpots can include liver and bacon, or fish, usually pilchards. When times were hard, just vegetables fried in fat would be used.

Lancashire Hotpot

500 g braising steak, trimmed of fat

250 g shoulder of lamb, trimmed of fat

2 lamb's kidneys, cleaned and trimmed (optional)

1 tablespoon plain flour

2 tablespoons beef dripping or butter (optional)

1 onion, thinly sliced

1 carrot, cut into chunks

1 bay leaf

300 ml beef stock (page 136) or water

½ teaspoon salt

1 teaspoon sugar

¼ teaspoon freshly ground black pepper

1 teaspoon anchovy essence or sauce

350 g potatoes, cut into walnut-sized chunks

SERVES 4

Cut the meats into 3 cm pieces and sprinkle with the flour. Mix well, then shake off the excess flour through a large sieve. Arrange the meats in a flameproof casserole. If preferred, heat the dripping or butter in a frying pan, add the vegetables and sauté until lightly browned. Transfer the vegetables, whether browned or not, to the casserole. Add the bay leaf, season the boiling stock or water with the salt, sugar, pepper and anchovy essence, then pour over the meats.

Cover, bring to the boil on top of the stove, then transfer to a preheated oven at 180°C (350°F) Gas 4 and simmer for 1 hour.

Arrange the potatoes, rounded side up, on top of the meats and spoon some of the meat juices over the top to glaze. Cover and return the casserole to the oven for a further hour. Remove the lid to allow the potatoes to become lightly browned and, increasing the heat if necessary, cook for a further 30 minutes.

A 'tian' is a shallow clay dish in the language of Provence and also any dish cooked in it. Overlapping layers of vegetables are arranged in the dish, then baked in the oven. Some vegetables, such as tomatoes and courgettes, are prone to throwing off a lot of liquid, so it's a good idea to remove some beforehand by roasting or salting (rather inelegantly known as 'degorging').

Provençal Tian

6 large ripe tomatoes, halved

4 garlic cloves, finely sliced

6 small aubergines, thickly sliced lengthways

3 green or yellow courgettes, thickly sliced lengthways

6 tablespoons olive oil, plus extra for brushing

2 large red onions, thickly sliced

2 tablespoons chopped fresh thyme leaves

sea salt and freshly ground black pepper

TOPPING

grated zest of 1 lemon

3 garlic cloves, crushed

about 140 g dried breadcrumbs

6 tablespoons freshly grated Parmesan cheese

sprigs of basil, to serve (optional)

SERVES 4–6

Put the tomatoes on a baking sheet, cut side up, and push slivers of garlic into each one. Roast in a preheated oven at 200°C (400°F) Gas 6 for about 30 minutes to remove some of the moisture.

Put the sliced aubergines and courgettes on a plate, sprinkle with salt and set aside for 30 minutes to extract some of the moisture. Rinse and pat dry with kitchen paper.

Heat the oil in a large frying pan, add the onion and sauté until softened and translucent. Remove from the pan and spread over the base of a tian or other shallow ceramic ovenproof dish.

Arrange overlapping layers of the tomatoes, aubergines and courgettes on top – arrange them in lines across the dish, like fish scales. Tuck the chopped thyme between the layers.

Brush with the extra olive oil and cook in a preheated oven at 200°C (400°F) Gas 6 for 20 minutes.

Meanwhile, to make the topping, grate the lemon zest into a bowl, add the crushed garlic and mix well. Stir in the breadcrumbs and cheese, then sprinkle over the top of the tian. Continue cooking for at least 30 minutes or until browned, finishing under the grill if necessary. Serve topped with basil leaves, if using.

The Moroccan tagine is one of the world's archetypal casseroles, both as a recipe and as a cooking pot. Made of glazed earthenware, this pot with a conical lid is placed over a brazier of hot coals – you see food stalls in the souks with small individual brazier-tagine combos bubbling all morning in preparation for the lunchtime onslaught. Traditionally, the only ovens are owned by bakers and used by householders to cook home-made bread and not, as is the custom in Italy, to simmer stews or slow-roasted meats.

Just as many food words in the countries ranging from Northern India to the Middle East and North Africa seem to have similar origins, so, too, many of the regional dishes have similar themes. Some authorities claim that Persia (now Iran) was the wellspring for some of the best-known dishes of the region, while others regard Turkey as more influential. Certainly, there is a common theme from Morocco to North India (the Indian lamb dish on page 95 is a recognizable relation of the Persian lamb on page 80 or the Turkish lamb on page 82).

Lamb, chicken and game appear most often in casseroles – because the whole region is predominantly Muslim, there are no pork dishes and not much beef. Above all, there is a delicious variety of vegetables and interesting ways of cooking them – as side dishes, pickles and in casseroles with rice or couscous.

The use of nuts and dried fruits, plus spices such as saffron and cinnamon, to flavour casseroles is one of the indications of Arab or Persian influence in cooking, wherever it appears.

AFRICA
AND THE
MIDDLE EAST

Chicken Tagine
with Quinces and Preserved Lemons

A tagine is the Moroccan clay cooking pot with a conical lid, and also any dish cooked in it. The shape encourages steam to rise into the lid, then drop back onto the meat, keeping it moist. Tagines often include fruits of various kinds, but the elegant, scented quince is a favourite in Morocco in the autumn. When unavailable, slightly unripe pears can be used instead, as they belong to the same botanical family. Preserved lemons add a salty tang: buy them in Middle Eastern food stores or make your own.

1 teaspoon ground saffron

2 cm fresh ginger, peeled and grated, or 1 teaspoon ground ginger

1½ tablespoons paprika

1 teaspoon freshly ground black pepper

2 teaspoons ground cinnamon

1 chicken, cut into 8 pieces

125 ml olive oil

2 large onions, grated

a pinch of saffron threads, soaked in boiling water for 30 minutes

6 garlic cloves, crushed

2 cinnamon sticks, broken in half

6 cloves

10 cardamom pods, lightly crushed

2 quinces, cored and cut into wedges

2 preserved lemons (optional)

coriander leaves, to serve

SERVES 4

Put the ground saffron, ginger, paprika, pepper and ground cinnamon in a bowl and mix well. Rub the chicken pieces in the mixture, put in a bowl, cover with clingfilm and marinate for at least 30 minutes or overnight in the refrigerator.

Heat the olive oil in a heavy-based casserole. Add the chicken and fry on all sides until golden. Add the onion, then the saffron threads and their soaking liquid, the garlic, cinnamon sticks, cloves and cardamom pods. Add 125 ml water and bring to the boil on top of the stove. Cover and simmer on top of the stove or in a preheated oven at 150°C (300°F) Gas 2 for 45 minutes, or until part-cooked.

Peel the quince wedges, add to the tagine and continue cooking for another 30 minutes or until the chicken is done and the quinces are tender.

If using preserved lemons, cut them in quarters and scrape off and discard the flesh. Cut the peel into thick slices lengthways and stir into the tagine. Heat for about 5–10 minutes, then serve the tagine sprinkled with coriander leaves.

Poussins
stuffed with Saffron Couscous

Although the couscous in this recipe is designed to be used as a stuffing, it is also delicious eaten on its own as a light lunch dish – albeit a shade sweet for the average tooth. The couscous sold in packets in the supermarket is precooked, so it only needs the correct amount of boiling water to be added to make it swell and yet stay fluffy when tossed with a fork. Too much water is disastrous and turns the mixture into a wet porridge. The delicious dried fruits and nuts used in the stuffing are typical of Muslim cooking and are found from Morocco to North India.

Poussins
stuffed with Saffron Couscous

step-by-step

a large pinch of saffron threads

1 onion, chopped

¼ teaspoon white pepper

3 tablespoons butter

1 cinnamon stick

4 poussins or 2 medium chickens

1 teaspoon honey

1 teaspoon ground cinnamon

sea salt

SAFFRON COUSCOUS STUFFING

70 g butter

100 g couscous

1 teaspoon salt

2 tablespoons orange flower water or a long curl of tangerine zest

100 g seedless raisins

80 g chopped almonds

2½ tablespoons sugar

2 teaspoons ground cinnamon

SERVES 4

1 To make the stuffing, heat half the butter in a large frying pan, then add the couscous and salt. Pour on 300 ml water, cover and bring to the boil.

2 Set aside for about 10 minutes, or until well puffed up, then fluff with a fork to separate the grains.

5 Put the saffron, onion, pepper, butter and cinnamon stick into a large, flameproof casserole, add 250 ml water and bring to the boil. Simmer for 2 minutes.

6 Lightly sprinkle the poussins inside and out with salt, then divide the stuffing into 4 portions and use to fill the cavities, packing it in very firmly.

3 Put the orange flower water in a saucepan, add the raisins and bring to the boil. Turn off the heat and set aside to absorb the liquid. If using tangerine zest instead, add 2 tablespoons water as well.

4 Put the almonds into a dry frying pan and toast over medium heat until golden.

5 Transfer the almonds to the couscous, then stir in the raisins, sugar, ground cinnamon and the remaining butter.

7 Truss the birds with string to keep the stuffing in place.

8 Stand the poussins close together in the casserole, breasts down, spooning some of the saffron mixture over the top. Bring to the boil, cover and simmer for 20 minutes, then turn them onto their sides and simmer for a further 20 minutes. Repeat this for a third time.

9 Prick the thighs with a fork – the juices should run clear. If not, cook for a further 10–20 minutes. When done, discard the string and put the birds on a serving platter. Add the honey and ground cinnamon to the juices in the pan, bring to the boil to make a thickish gravy, then pour over the birds and serve.

Persian Lamb Khoresh
with Saffron Chelo Rice

The rice needs a bit of practice to get it right, with a crust on the bottom (called *tak dip*), but not to have it burnt irrevocably onto the bottom of the pan. Try cheating with a non-stick one.

2 aubergines, peeled and quartered lengthways

1 tablespoon salt

125 g clarified butter (page 83)

3 onions, finely sliced

1 kg boneless lamb, such as shoulder, cut into 2 cm cubes

1 teaspoon ground turmeric

½ teaspoon crushed black pepper

4 tomatoes, skinned and deseeded

250 g spinach

350 g dried fruits, such as pitted dates, ready-to-eat dried apricots, dried apples or figs, chopped if large

freshly squeezed juice of 1 lime, plus lime wedges, to serve

sea salt and freshly ground black pepper

SAFFRON CHELO RICE

500 g basmati rice

½ teaspoon salt

125 g butter

a large pinch of saffron threads

SERVES 4

Sprinkle the aubergine wedges with the salt and set aside for 2 hours to draw out some of the liquid. Rinse well to remove the salt and pat dry with kitchen paper.

Heat the clarified butter in a flameproof casserole, add the aubergine wedges and fry until thoroughly browned on all sides. Remove with a slotted spoon, put on a plate and keep them warm.

Add the onions to the casserole and fry gently until softened and browned. Remove with a slotted spoon and add to the plate of aubergines.

Add a little more butter if necessary, then add the lamb cubes and sprinkle with the turmeric and pepper. Sauté, turning the pieces, until browned on all sides.

Return the onions to the pan, then add the tomatoes. Add water to cover and salt and pepper to taste. Bring to the boil, reduce the heat and simmer gently for 30 minutes, or until the lamb is half-cooked. Add the aubergines, spinach and dried fruits. Continue simmering for 30 minutes, or until the lamb is tender. Taste and adjust the seasoning with a little lime juice. Serve with the Chelo Rice and lime wedges.

Saffron Chelo Rice

Put the rice in a bowl, cover with plenty of cold water and soak for at least 2 hours, or overnight. Drain well.

Fill a large saucepan with water, add the salt, bring to the boil and trickle in the rice slowly so that the water never stops boiling. Cook for 10 minutes. Drain.

Put the butter in a frying pan with lid, add 500 ml water and heat until the butter has melted. Pour off half the butter water into a measuring jug. Add the rice to the pan and cook quickly, so that it sticks to the base of the pan, about 1 minute. Add the rest of the butter water and the saffron threads, cover the pan and cook over a very gentle heat for about 30 minutes, or until all the water has been absorbed and the base has dried out again.

Serve from the pan or turn it out onto a platter: the crisp, slightly burnt rice from the bottom of the pan is highly prized.

Note Like most casseroles, this one is delicious cooled and chilled. The following day, crack any fat off the top and discard it, then reheat the lamb before serving (page 142).

Turkish Lamb
with Butternuts and Courgettes

Turkey, like Iran, loves butter – soup, for instance is often topped with butter melted with paprika. For frying, the butter should be clarified, so the milky residue is drained out so that it cannot burn and taint the dish. The easiest way to clarify butter is to cut a block into slices, put into a bowl, cover with clingfilm and microwave on HIGH for 1½ minutes. Let it settle for 2 minutes, then pour off the clear oil and discard the residue. Store in the refrigerator.

2 teaspoons ground cinnamon

2 teaspoons paprika

2 garlic cloves, crushed

1 teaspoon virgin olive oil

1 kg lamb shoulder, cubed

125 g clarified butter (see recipe introduction)

2 onions, sliced

1 aubergine, peeled and sliced

1 red pepper, deseeded and cut into 8 strips

1 yellow or orange pepper, deseeded and cut into 8 strips

4 tomatoes, skinned, halved and deseeded

½ butternut squash, cut into 1 cm cubes

500 g baby new potatoes, about 20

125 g green beans, topped and tailed

65 g okra, minimally trimmed at the stalk end

2 medium courgettes, cut into thick chunks

sea salt and freshly ground black pepper

SERVES 4

Put the cinnamon, paprika, garlic and oil in a small bowl, mix well, then rub the meat with the paste. Let marinate in the refrigerator for about 30 minutes while you prepare the vegetables.

Heat the clarified butter in a flameproof casserole, add the onion and fry until softened and browned. Remove the onion from the casserole, add the meat and fry until browned on all sides, about 10 minutes. Return the onion to the pan.

Add enough water to cover and season with plenty of salt and pepper. Bring to the boil, reduce the heat and simmer for 40 minutes, until the meat begins to tenderize.

Tuck in the aubergine, peppers, tomatoes, butternut cubes and potatoes, adding more water if necessary.

Taste and adjust the seasoning if necessary, cover with a lid, bring to the boil, then transfer to a preheated oven and simmer at 170°C (325°F) Gas 3 until vegetables and meat are tender, about 40 minutes. Add the green beans, okra and courgettes for the last 10 minutes of cooking.

The colours in this casserole are only equalled by its flavour. Both are startling and gorgeous. Don't overdo the harissa – just a little will just wake you up. Let the vegetables char and acquire a bit of barbecue flavour – and don't forget the yoghurt.

North African Charred Vegetables

3 red onions, cut into wedges

18 cherry tomatoes

1 large courgette, cut into wedges

150 g small red potatoes, halved

2 red peppers, deseeded and cut into strips or wedges

1 yellow pepper, deseeded and cut into strips or wedges

2 fennel bulbs, cut in wedges

6 tablespoons olive oil

6 garlic cloves, crushed to a paste

½ teaspoon harissa paste

1 teaspoon ground cumin

1 tablespoon vinegar

1 tablespoon chopped fresh mint

1 tablespoon chopped fresh coriander

2 teaspoons sea salt

500 ml Greek yoghurt, to serve

SERVES 4–6

Reserve 1 onion and 4 cherry tomatoes. Arrange the remaining vegetables in a roasting tin, drizzle with 4 tablespoons of the oil and roast in a preheated oven at 250°C (475°F) Gas 9 or the highest temperature available on your stove until they begin to char, about 30 minutes.

Lower the heat to 180°C (350°F) Gas 4. Remove the vegetables from the oven and transfer to a shallow casserole dish.

Put the crushed garlic in a small bowl and mash in the harissa, cumin and remaining oil. Stir in the vinegar, mint and coriander. Mix this in with the vegetables, tuck in the last onion and 4 cherry tomatoes, sprinkle generously with salt and return the casserole to the oven to bake for a further 25 minutes.

If there is too much liquid, pour it off into a small saucepan, bring to the boil and simmer until reduced and concentrated in flavour. Pour back into the casserole. Serve with lashings of yoghurt.

Is curry a casserole? In India there's no such thing as 'curry' or 'curry powder'. What we think of as curry comes in countless different varieties, from stir-fries to casseroles, according to region, community or religion. Curry powder was invented for British ex-pats, who returned home to find that they missed the gorgeous spice mixes or masalas of the East, but it is a pale, flavourless imitation of the real thing.

The making of a masala is a very skilled business: every bride is given a spice box or *masala dani,* from which she blends her own mixtures into an infinite variety of flavours, different for each dish, and carefully handed down from mother to daughter.

The masala spices and flavourings are pounded, blended and made into a paste or powder, then toasted to mature their flavours and release their oils before the next stage of cooking. In many dishes, the next step is to add ghee or oil, then the 'trinity' of onion, garlic and fresh ginger. Meat, poultry or vegetables are added and simmered until done. Dishes are often then 'tempered' – topped with a spicy fried onion mixture – before serving.

Most foods are cooked over direct heat, such as hot coals or an open stove. Closed ovens are not usual in domestic kitchens in this part of the world. However, in larger establishments, such as royal kitchens or big hotels, methods closer to oven-cooking of casseroles are sometimes seen. For instance, in the *dum pukht* cooking from the northern city of Lucknow, the spiced dish is transferred to a lidded pot and the whole is sealed with a rim of dough and allowed to cook gently in its own steam and juices, rather like a French daube.

INDIA

Fish Mollee

A *mollee* is a South Indian sauce, one of those dishes known wrongly in the rest of the world as a 'curry'. It is mostly used for poaching fish, but is also delicious as a medium for reheating cooked meats or vegetables. The first step is to make the sauce: after that, you may add what you like. In the south, this is often served with great mounds of fluffy rice flavoured with cumin seed. In India, dishes such as this are cooked in the Indian wok, called a *karahi*.

500 g firm fish such as salmon, monkfish or cod

1 tablespoon ground turmeric

1 teaspoon salt

100 g ghee (clarified butter), butter or sunflower oil

1 onion, chopped

1 garlic clove, crushed

2 small fresh green chillies, deseeded if preferred, then chopped

3 cm fresh ginger, peeled and grated

12 cardamom pods, crushed

6 cloves, crushed

1 cinnamon stick, about 5 cm

500 ml canned coconut milk

freshly squeezed lemon juice, to taste

torn fresh coriander leaves, to serve

SERVES 4

Cut the fish into 3 cm strips. Mix the turmeric and salt on a plate, roll the fish in the mixture and set aside for a few minutes.

Meanwhile, heat the ghee, butter or oil in a flameproof casserole or large saucepan. Add the onion, garlic, chillies, ginger, cardamom, cloves and cinnamon stick and sauté until the onion is softened and translucent.

Add the coconut milk, heat until simmering and cook until the mixture is quite thick. Add the fish to the casserole, then spoon the sauce over the top, making sure the fish is well covered. Cook for 10 minutes on top of the stove or in a preheated oven at 150°C (300°F) Gas 2, until the fish is opaque all the way through. Serve sprinkled with lemon juice and coriander.

Kerala, on the south-west coast of India, is coconut country – and one of the great spice producing areas of the world (it was famous as such even in ancient times). It has a marvellous tradition of vegetarian cooking and an inspired touch with seafood.

Kerala Coconut Chilli Prawns

250 g spinach, well washed

100 g green beans

50 g ghee or peanut oil

2 onions, chopped

3 garlic cloves, chopped

3 cm fresh ginger, peeled and chopped

2 green chillies, deseeded and chopped

1 tablespoon ground cumin

1 teaspoon freshly ground black pepper

6 green cardamom pods, crushed

2 cloves

a pinch of salt

freshly squeezed juice of ½ lemon

500 ml thick coconut milk

500 g peeled, uncooked prawns

3 tablespoons chopped fresh coriander

TO SERVE (OPTIONAL)

3–4 green chillies, sliced

a handful of coriander leaves

SERVES 4

Bring a large saucepan of water to the boil and plunge in the spinach for 20 seconds. Remove with a slotted spoon and refresh under cold running water to stop the cooking process; squeeze out as much water as possible. Set aside. Add the beans and cook just until crunchy, about 3 minutes. Drain, refresh in cold water, drain again and add to the spinach.

Heat the ghee or oil in an ovenproof casserole, add the onion, garlic, ginger and chillies and fry until soft. Add the cumin, pepper, cardamom, cloves, salt and 1 teaspoon of the lemon juice and cook for 5 minutes.

Stir in the coconut milk. Add the beans and prawns, then stir in the chopped coriander and the rest of the lemon juice. Cook in a preheated oven at 150°C (300°F) Gas 2 for about 25 minutes, or until the prawns have just become opaque. Add the spinach for the last 5 minutes to reheat. Do not overcook or the prawns will be tough and tasteless.

Sprinkle with the sliced green chillies and a handful of coriander leaves, then serve with plain rice or rice mixed with pan-toasted cumin seeds.

Saffron and Pistachio Biryani

The biryani is a Muslim dish, often linked with the 'gourmet' city of Hyderabad, and especially popular in North India and Pakistan. It often includes chicken or lamb, but a vegetarian version is also delicious. For celebrations, it may have gold or silver leaf on top.

a large pinch of saffron threads

2½ teaspoons salt

200 g butter ghee (clarified butter)

600 ml basmati rice, measured by volume

2 cinnamon sticks

6 cloves

2 bay leaves

6 green cardamom pods, crushed

1 tablespoon ground cumin

½ onion, sliced

3 cm fresh ginger, peeled and sliced

2 red chillies, deseeded and sliced

3 garlic cloves, crushed

4 chicken breasts, skinned and boned

250 ml plain yoghurt, strained, or Greek yoghurt

1 tablespoon chopped fresh mint

1 tablespoon lightly chopped coriander

TO SERVE

½ onion, fried till crisp, then crumbled

50 g green pistachio nuts, shelled, blanched and peeled

30 g almonds, toasted in a dry frying pan, then sliced

50 g raisins or sultanas, soaked in 2 tablespoons boiling water for 30 minutes

a handful of coriander leaves

SERVES 4

Put the saffron into a large saucepan with 150 ml water and ½ teaspoon of the salt. Bring to the boil, then set aside to cool.

Melt 75 g of the ghee in a second saucepan. Add the rice and fry gently, stirring continuously, until the rice is white and opaque, about 5 minutes. Add 1 litre water, 1 teaspoon salt, 1 cinnamon stick, 3 cloves, 1 bay leaf and half the cardamom. Cover with a lid, bring to the boil, reduce the heat and simmer until all the water has been absorbed, about 10–15 minutes. (The rice will be slightly undercooked.)

Measure 600 ml by volume of this part-cooked rice and add to the pan of saffron water. Stir well, cover with a lid, bring to the boil and cook for a couple of minutes or until the rice has absorbed all the water.

Add 100 ml water to the remaining white rice, stir, cover, bring to the boil and cook for a couple of minutes or until the rice has absorbed all the water.

Measure a further 600 ml of this rice and mix it gently with the saffron rice to give a yellow and white mixture.

Spread the remaining white rice into an a shallow casserole dish and set aside.

Rinse out the saucepan, add the remaining 125 g ghee and heat gently. Stir in the remaining cardamom, cloves, cinnamon stick, bay leaf and the ground cumin and fry to release the spice aroma.

Meanwhile, put the onion, ginger, chillies, garlic and 5 tablespoons water in a blender and purée until smooth. Pour this mixture into the pan of hot spices and heat until the water has boiled away and the ghee begins to fry the mixture.

Add the chicken and seal all over without browning it or the spices. Add the yoghurt, mint, coriander and remaining salt and cover with a lid. Raise the heat and simmer, without boiling, for 20 minutes. (Don't worry when the sauce appears to split and become buttery.)

Remove the chicken and arrange on top of the rice in the casserole, pour the yoghurt sauce over, cover and cook in a preheated oven at 190°C (375°F) Gas 5 for about 20 minutes while the rice absorbs the liquid.

Remove from the oven and arrange the bi-coloured rice on top, then return it to the oven for a further 5 minutes to heat through. Serve, topped with the onion, nuts, raisins and coriander leaves.

Spiced Lamb
with Coconut

A gentle casserole 'curry' with plenty of flavour, especially if you can marinate it overnight. The recipe comes from Gujerat, one of the north-western states of India, and it shows several typical methods of cooking casserole dishes in the area. The Indian flavour 'trinity' of onions, garlic and ginger is stir-fried first, then a subtle combination of traditional spices is added and part-cooked to release their aromas. After the pieces of lamb have been added and cooked to tenderness, the dish is finished with a final 'tempering' of stir-fried onions and mustard seeds. Compare it with the lamb dishes in the Middle East chapter and you will notice how they are related. Serve the lamb with other Indian dishes, such as one of the spicy vegetable dishes (page 98), a dhaal (lentils), a chutney and rice or naan bread.

This recipe may also be adapted to the *dum pukht* cooking method originating in the royal kitchens of Lucknow, in the Central Indian state of Uttar Pradesh. At the end of cooking time, the dish is transferred to a lidded casserole, sealed with a ring of dough (or a sheet of foil), like a French daube, and steamed for 15 minutes.

Spiced Lamb
with Coconut

step-by-step

1 kg leg or shoulder of lamb,
boned and cubed

750 ml canned coconut milk

a handful of fresh coconut slivers
or 1 tablespoon desiccated coconut,
pan-toasted

a handful of coriander leaves, fresh methi
(fenugreek) or curry leaves, to serve

TEMPERING

2 tablespoons mustard oil or peanut oil

2 red onions, cut into wedges

2 tablespoons mustard seeds

SPICY MASALA PASTE

6 tablespoons peanut oil

3 onions, chopped

5 cm fresh ginger, peeled and grated

3 large garlic cloves, chopped

1 teaspoon ground cinnamon

1 tablespoon ground cumin

1 tablespoon ground coriander

¼ teaspoon ground cardamom

1 teaspoon ground turmeric

2 teaspoons dried chilli flakes

3 tablespoons vinegar

1 teaspoon salt

SERVES 4

1 To make the masala paste, heat the oil in a karahi (wok), frying pan or metal casserole dish, add the onions, ginger and garlic and stir-fry until lightly browned.

2 Add the cinnamon, cumin, ground coriander, cardamom, turmeric and chilli flakes and cook until the fragrance is released, about 3–4 minutes.

Variation

Lamb Dum Pukht Follow the main recipe, using Greek yoghurt instead of coconut milk, to step 5. For the last 10 minutes of cooking time, transfer the contents of the pan to a lidded casserole dish. Make a simple dough of flour and water and roll out to a 2.5 cm thick sausage, long enough to fit around the rim of your casserole. Press the dough on top of the rim, then press the lid on top to make a tight seal. Alternatively, press a sheet of foil on top, then put on the lid. Cook in a preheated oven at 200°C (400°F) Gas 5 for 15 minutes. Break open the seal at the table – the aroma is wonderful.

3 Stir in the vinegar and salt.

4 Add the lamb to the pan and fry, turning frequently, for about 10 minutes until lightly browned on all sides. At this point, you may remove it from the heat, let cool, then chill overnight to marinate and develop the flavours (if time is short, this step may be omitted).

5 Add about 600 ml of the coconut milk. Add water to cover, heat to simmering, then cook until the meat is tender, about 40 minutes. Stir from time to time to prevent the mixture from sticking to the pan. Stir in the rest of the coconut milk and cook for a further 10 minutes.

6 Meanwhile, put the coconut in a dry karahi or frying pan and stir-fry for a few minutes until lightly golden: take care, the pieces can easily burn. Set aside.

7 To make the tempering, heat the oil in a karahi or frying pan, add the onion and mustard seeds and stir-fry until the onion is softened and dark golden brown around the edges. Remove from the heat.

8 Transfer the lamb to a serving dish, spoon the tempering over the top and the coconut on top of that. Add the coriander, fresh methi or curry leaves, if using, and serve with other Indian dishes.

Dum Aloo
Steamed Spicy Potatoes

This is Indian comfort food: I could eat it by the bucketful. *Dum* means 'steam' and *aloo* means 'potatoes' in this steam-fry method of Indian casserole cooking. It is usually served with a number of other dishes: a dhaal (lentil), perhaps three chutneys – one sweet, one spicy and one sour – plus rice (in the south) or naan bread (in the north). It is also rolled up in the delicious crispy pancake called a dosa to form a masala dosa. But this dish doesn't have to be Indian: serve it with any meat or poultry dishes.

500 g baby potatoes or medium ones cut into chunks

2 tablespoons shelled green peas (optional)

3 tablespoons ghee or peanut oil (never olive oil)

1 onion, chopped

2 garlic cloves, crushed

3 cm fresh ginger, peeled and grated

1 tablespoon ground cumin

1 tablespoon ground coriander or 2 tablespoons coriander seeds, crushed

2 teaspoons dried chilli flakes, or 2 fresh chillies, deseeded if preferred, then chopped

2 tomatoes, skinned, halved and deseeded

12 spinach leaves (optional)

salt, to taste

SERVES 4

Cook the potatoes in boiling salted water until part-cooked. Drain. Cook the peas, if using, in the same way.

Heat the ghee or oil in a lidded casserole dish, add the onion, garlic and ginger and stir-fry until golden brown. Add the salt and spices and cook until they become aromatic, about 5 minutes.

Add the tomatoes, bring to the boil, reduce the heat, then simmer to a purée. Add the potatoes, mix gently to cover with the onion mixture, then cover with a lid and simmer until done, about 20 minutes. If using peas or spinach, add them for the last 2–3 minutes of cooking time.

Chickpeas
with Mustard Seeds

125 g dried chickpeas or 2 cans, about 480 g when rinsed and drained

1 tablespoon peanut or mustard oil

2 teaspoons ground turmeric

2 teaspoons black mustard seeds

2 onions, chopped

2 garlic cloves, chopped

1 tablespoon dried fenugreek leaves (optional)

4 tomatoes, skinned, halved and deseeded

3–5 fresh red chillies, halved, deseeded if preferred, then chopped

salt, to taste

fresh methi leaves, to serve (optional)*

SERVES 4

Dried fenugreek leaves (known as 'methi' in India and some Asian spice shops) are not as easy to find as the seeds, but they have a unique flavour which scents the dish and makes it something out of the ordinary. If you can't find it in your spice shop, use mint instead, or omit altogether. Use enough chillies to suit your taste.

Put the chickpeas in a bowl, add cold water to cover and let soak overnight. Next day, drain, put in a flameproof casserole dish, bring to the boil, then transfer to a preheated oven and cook at 150°C (300°F) Gas 2 for about 2 hours, or until tender (the time will depend on the age of the chickpeas). Add salt, simmer for a further 10 minutes, then drain. If using canned chickpeas, rinse and drain them well.

Heat the oil in the casserole, add the turmeric and mustard seeds and heat until the seeds pop. Add the onions and garlic and fry gently until softened and lightly browned. Add the dried fenugreek leaves, if using, tomatoes and chillies. Cook at a low heat until the tomatoes have melted down to form a sauce.

Return the chickpeas to the casserole, turn to coat with the mixture, cook until hot, then serve, topped with sprigs of fresh methi leaves, if using.

Note Fresh methi leaves are sold in Indian greengrocers. They are cooked and served a little like spinach, but a few sprigs make a delicious garnish. Omit if they are hard to find.

The countries of East and South-east Asia are as diverse in their cooking styles as Denmark is from Italy or Russia from Spain, so it is remarkable that any similarity exists. But it does: it is especially the cooking methods that unite them, as well as the use of spices, sometimes used sparingly and sometimes vigorously.

Traditionally, ovens are rare and slow casserole cooking is still done on top of a source of heat. In the popular Chinese method of 'red cooking' or *hoong sui*, whole joints of pork or entire fowl are immersed in a pan of highly soy-seasoned liquid and poached gently.

The traditional sandpot is the most recognizable casserole dish in the region. Fairly fragile, it is an earthenware container, glazed inside, and often bound outside with wire to give it strength. Placed directly above hot charcoal, the contents are brought to simmering point and left to cook, often for several hours. A word of warning, however: a naked gas flame, even turned to its lowest, is too violent a source of heat and will crack the pot, so a heat diffuser is essential. Using a sandpot in an ordinary oven is a much safer bet.

Chinese *dumm* steaming is an even slower form of cooking. Meats are first seared in a wok, flavourings added and the whole turned out into a lidded pot, which is placed on a trivet and lowered into a pan half-filled with hot water which can simmer away all day. This is reminiscent of the French bain-marie way of cooking, showing that a good idea is a good idea anywhere.

Alas, this chapter can only provide a tantalizing taste of the casseroles dishes and cooking methods from this part of the world: I hope they inspire you to search further.

EAST AND SOUTH-EAST ASIA

Green Thai Fish Curry

Thai curries are easy to make, quick to cook and totally delicious. The secret is in the mixture of spices and the freshness of the pastes. You can make the paste in a food processor using ground spices or, if you prefer using whole ones, break them down in a coffee grinder kept solely for that purpose. Store unused paste in the refrigerator.

400 ml coconut milk

750 g fish fillets, such as monkfish, cod, John Dory or other firm fish

1 tablespoon peanut oil

SPICE PASTE

1 onion, sliced

3 garlic cloves, chopped

6 small hot green chillies, deseeded and sliced

5 cm fresh ginger, peeled or scraped and sliced

1 teaspoon ground white pepper

1 teaspoon ground coriander

½ teaspoon ground turmeric

½ teaspoon ground cumin

1 teaspoon shrimp paste (belacan)

1 tablespoon fish sauce

1 stalk of lemongrass, peeled and finely sliced

TO SERVE:

sprigs of Thai basil (optional)

2 limes, halved

fragrant Thai rice or noodles

SERVES 4

Put all the spice paste ingredients in a food processor and work them into a fine purée. Alternatively, use a mortar and pestle. Set aside.

Put the oil in a wok and heat well. Add the spice paste and stir-fry for a few seconds to release the aromas. Add the thick portion from the top of the coconut milk, stir well and boil to thicken a little.

Add the fish and turn the pieces over in the sauce until they are well coated. Reheat to simmering and cook just until they start to become opaque, about 2 minutes.

Add the remaining coconut milk and continue cooking until the fish is cooked through. Serve topped with Thai basil, if using, plus the halved limes and fragrant Thai rice or noodles.

Note Thai and Vietnamese basil is quite different from ordinary basil. It is sold in Asian food markets – omit it if you can't find it.

Malay Chicken Noodle Soup

2 bundles beanthread or rice noodles such as *ho-fun* or *bahn-pho*, fresh or dried

1.5 litres Asian chicken stock (pages 138-9) or water

1.5 kg whole chicken or 750 g boneless, skinless chicken breasts

about 250 g green beans or Chinese yard-long beans, cut into 7 cm lengths

1 carrot, finely sliced

1 courgette, finely sliced

2 tablespoons peanut oil

sea salt and freshly ground black pepper

SPICE PASTE

2 stalks of lemongrass

2 tablespoons black pepper, coarsely cracked

2 tablespoons fish sauce, or 1 teaspoon shrimp paste (belacan)

2 teaspoons ground turmeric

8 pink Thai shallots or 2 brown onions, finely chopped

3 cm fresh ginger, peeled and grated

6 garlic cloves, crushed

a large handful of blanched almonds

TO SERVE

baby mushrooms, such as enokitaki or hon-shimeji, separated (optional)

4 spring onions, finely sliced

4 red chillies, finely sliced

2 lemons, cut in wedges

SERVES 4

You find soups like this in Malaysia, Indonesia and other parts of South-east Asia. Use a whole chicken to make the stock, then remove the skin and bone and shred the meat. Alternatively, use ready-made stock and poach chicken breasts separately. Use beanthread or rice vermicelli noodles, not wheat-based ones. Any number of vegetables may be added. You can use a ready-made Thai spice paste, but a blender makes this one in a minute.

If using dried noodles, put them in a bowl and cover with hot water. Let soak for about 30 minutes, then drain and keep in cold water until ready to serve. If using fresh noodles, cut or separate them into strips, soak in hot water for a few minutes, then drain and keep in cold water until ready to serve.

Put the stock or water in a stockpot and bring to the boil. Add the chicken – add more boiling water if the bird is not completely covered by liquid. Poach gently until the chicken is tender, about 1 hour. Remove the chicken to a plate, let cool slightly, discard the skin and bones, then shred the flesh into long pieces. If using chicken breasts, bring the stock to the boil, add the chicken breasts and poach gently until tender, about 15 minutes. Remove from the stock and shred. Return the stock to the boil, add the beans and carrots and simmer for 5 minutes or until al dente. Remove with a slotted spoon and plunge them into a bowl of iced water to arrest the cooking. Add the courgette to the stock and blanch gently until tender, about 1 minute. Remove with a slotted spoon and add to the bowl of iced water. Reserve the stock. When all the vegetables are cold, remove them from the iced water and reserve.

To make the spice paste, cut the top off the lemongrass, keeping the white part only. Peel off the 2 outer leaves, and finely slice the rest. Put in a small blender or food processor with the other spice paste ingredients and grind to a coarse paste. Alternatively, use a mortar and pestle. Set aside.

Heat the oil in a wok or frying pan, add the spice paste and fry gently until fragrant. Add the reserved stock, shredded chicken, blanched beans, carrots and courgettes and heat until very hot. Taste and adjust the seasoning. Drain the noodles and divide between 4 large bowls. Ladle the chicken and stock over the noodles and serve, topped with the spring onions, chillies and mushrooms, if using. Serve with lemon wedges for squeezing.

A recipe from the border of China and the former Indo-China – the tang of orange mixed with crushed yellow bean sauce is a gorgeous combination and the whole dish can be prepared in advance up to the point where it is put in the oven. A word of warning – the sauce around the duck, before it is put into the oven, must be very thick, because the bok choy or cabbage gives off so much water that the dish can easily become diluted.

Braised Duck and Ginger

4 large duck breasts, cut into thick slices

5 teaspoons cornflour

4 tablespoons yellow bean paste or sauce

2 tablespoons Shaohsing (sweet Chinese rice wine) or mirin

2 teaspoons sugar

freshly ground black pepper

1 onion, finely chopped

2 tablespoons peanut oil

10 cm fresh ginger, peeled and thickly sliced

2 garlic cloves, crushed

zest of 1 orange or 1 tangerine

2 tablespoons dark soy sauce

4 baby bok choy, halved lengthways, or ½ Chinese cabbage, sliced crossways

4 spring onions, sliced, to serve

SERVES 4

Put the duck in a bowl, sprinkle with 1 teaspoon of the cornflour and mix until coated.

Heat a wok or frying pan, add the duck (without adding any oil) and stir-fry to release the fat and firm up the meat. Remove with a slotted spoon and return the duck to the bowl.

Put the bean paste or sauce in a small bowl, add 125 ml water, the rice wine or mirin, sugar and freshly ground black pepper and mix well.

Add the onion to the wok or pan, then add the bean paste mixture. Simmer for about 30 seconds, then pour the mixture over the duck. Reheat the wok with the oil and sauté the ginger and garlic to release their flavour. Return the duck and its sauce to the wok, add the zest and simmer lightly until most of the water has evaporated.

Mix the remaining cornflour with 2 tablespoons water and the soy sauce, stir into the wok and bring to the boil, stirring.

Line a Chinese sandpot with the bok choy or Chinese cabbage, arrange the duck over the top, then pour over the sauce. Cook a preheated oven at 180°C (350°F) Gas 4 for 10 minutes until tender. Remove from the oven and, if the leaves have given off too much liquid, pour it into a saucepan or wok and boil until it thickens again to a coating consistency. Return to the pot, sprinkle with the spring onions and serve with other Chinese dishes.

'Red-cooking' is a braising method used for whole ducks or chickens, or large pieces of pork – and the red colour comes from soy sauce. This dish uses a great deal of soy, but it can be used again and again (freeze between uses). Use dark soy, which is less salty than light.

Red-cooked Pork

1 kg pork spareribs, loin or shoulder, in the piece

RED STOCK
500 ml Chinese rice wine
750 ml chicken stock or water
500 ml dark soy sauce
2 tablespoons rice vinegar
2 cinnamon sticks
3 cm fresh ginger, sliced
zest of 1 tangerine or orange
2 whole star anise
6 spring onions

SERVES 6–8

Put all the stock ingredients into a large flameproof casserole and bring to the boil. Add the pork, return to the boil, then simmer on top of the stove or in a preheated oven at 180°C (350°F) Gas 4 for 45 minutes if using pork loin, or 1½ hours if using pork shoulder or spareribs. When the meat is very tender, carefully lift it out onto on a wooden board and, using a Chinese cleaver, cut it into thick slices or bite-sized chunks. Serve with other Chinese dishes such as noodles, stir-fried vegetables or steamed rice.

Notes Some of the stock is served with the dish, the rest is kept and used over and over again, improving in flavour each time a new dish is cooked in it: if you don't plan to make this often, the stock may be frozen.

Although red-cooked pork is a typical Chinese dish – and perfect served with other Chinese dishes – it is also delicious served with mashed potatoes or mashed white beans, with a little of the stock drizzled over.

Variation For extra flavour, marinate the pork overnight in the refrigerator in a South-east Asian spice paste. Using a blender or mortar and pestle, grind 1 teaspoon ground coriander, 1 teaspoon crushed white peppercorns, 4 crushed garlic cloves, 2 stalks of lemongrass, peeled and chopped, 5 cm fresh ginger, peeled and chopped, 4 red chillies, deseeded and chopped, 2 teaspoon shrimp paste (optional), 1 tablespoon sunflower oil and 2 teaspoons rice vinegar. Spread the mixture over the pork and marinate overnight in the refrigerator.

Aubergine Sandpot

1 small aubergine or
4 Chinese aubergines

200 g broccoli

1½ teaspoons salt

1½ teaspoons sugar

1 carrot, cut in batons, or 8 baby
carrots, halved lengthways

3 tablespoons peanut oil

1 tablespoon sesame oil

3 cm fresh ginger, peeled and sliced

2 garlic cloves, crushed

about 240 g canned water chestnuts,
rinsed and drained

1 tablespoon yellow bean paste,
thinned with 6 tablespoons water

1 tablespoon dark soy sauce

1 tablespoon rice vinegar

125 ml vegetable stock

2 teaspoons cornflour,
mixed with 1 tablespoon water

2 spring onions, finely sliced

SERVES 4

If using a whole aubergine, trim and cut it into finger-sized strips. If using Chinese aubergines, halve them lengthways. Snap the florets off the broccoli, peel the stalk and cut it into finger-sized strips.

Bring a large saucepan of water to the boil, then add ½ teaspoon of the salt and ½ teaspoon of the sugar. Add the broccoli florets and boil for 2 minutes. Remove the florets with a slotted spoon and put into a bowl of cold water.

Add the broccoli stems and carrots to the boiling water and blanch for 5 minutes. Remove with a slotted spoon and add to the bowl of cold water. Drain the vegetables through a colander, reserving the cooking water.

Put the peanut oil and 1 teaspoon of the sesame oil in a wok or frying pan, add the ginger and garlic and stir-fry for 2 minutes. Add the drained vegetables and water chestnuts and stir-fry for 2 minutes to coat with the oil and make them glisten. Transfer to a sandpot or other casserole.

Add the remaining sesame oil to the wok, then add the diluted yellow bean paste, soy sauce, vinegar, stock, the remaining sugar and salt and 125 ml of the blanching water. Bring to the boil. Mix the cornflour with 1 tablespoon water, then stir into the wok.

Pour over the vegetables and sprinkle with sliced spring onions. Cover and transfer to a preheated oven at 350°F (180°C) Gas 4 and cook for 20 minutes or until the liquid bubbles through. Serve with other Chinese dishes.

Asian aubergines come in all shapes, sizes and colours. They range from tiny, green, grape-like bunches to the egg-shaped white ones which gave them one of their common names, 'eggplant' – and from the familiar large, purple kinds to the Chinese varieties, about 7 cm long, which are ideal for this recipe.

Monks' Vegetables

Vegetarian diets were never hugely popular in China. The monasteries were the main proponents of the vegetarian lifestyle – and there aren't many monks left in the People's Republic. However, I love this dish and I'm certainly not a vegetarian. It is so good that any meat would utterly ruin its flavour – and yet it has the satisfying effect of a meat dish. Fry the ingredients in the order given, so that you build up the pot in the recommended order. If you haven't got one ingredient, choose something similar so their textures give a good balance of crunch and softness. Make sure to give the beancurd a very light dusting of cornflour so the pieces will brown deliciously all over without sticking.

Monks' Vegetables
step-by-step

½ Chinese cabbage, leaves separated

250 ml peanut oil

4 carrots, peeled and finely sliced diagonally

240 g canned sliced bamboo shoots, drained

150 g fresh shiitake mushrooms, halved

240 g canned sliced water chestnuts, drained

4 baby bok choy, halved lengthways

2 blocks firm beancurd (tofu), cut into
3 cm cubes

3 tablespoons cornflour, for dusting

SAUCE

2 tablespoons crushed yellow bean sauce
diluted with 6 tablespoons water

2 tablespoons light soy sauce

2 tablespoons dark soy sauce

2 tablespoons hoisin sauce

2 tablespoons sugar

200 ml water or vegetable stock

125 ml Shaohsing (Chinese sweetened rice
wine) or medium sherry

SERVES 4

1 Bring a large saucepan of water to the boil, add the Chinese cabbage leaves and blanch for 1 minute. Remove, plunge into a large bowl of iced water, then drain.

2 Cut out and discard the white stalks. Put the leaves one on top of the other on a dry cloth (arrange them with stalk ends on alternate sides).

6 Dust the beancurd with the flour, in several batches (do this just before frying).

7 Heat 125 ml of the oil in the wok or frying pan (it must be very hot or the beancurd will stick). Fry the beancurd pieces in the oil until well browned. Remove with a slotted spoon, then drain.

3 Roll up the leaves like a sushi into a cylinder and press hard to squeeze out the water.

4 Remove from the cloth and cut the rolls into 5 cm lengths. Set aside.

Note This cabbage preparation is based on a Japanese original, but is a terrific way to include lots of leaves in the dish without taking up huge amounts of room.

5 Heat 1 tablespoon of the oil in a wok or frying pan until it begins to smoke. Stir-fry all the vegetables, except the cabbage and bok choy, one at a time in the order shown, removing each one to a plate before adding the next. Add more oil as required and reheat it each time before frying the next batch.

8 Put a layer of fried beancurd in a Chinese sandpot or ceramic casserole dish. Add the carrots, bamboo shoots, mushrooms, water chestnuts, bok choy and cabbage rolls.

9 Mix the sauce ingredients in a jug or bowl and pour over the vegetables. Cover with a lid and set aside to marinate for about 30 minutes or until you are ready to cook the final dish.

10 Put the sandpot or casserole into a cold oven, turn the heat to 200°C (400°F) Gas 6 for about 20 minutes, or until boiling, then reduce the heat to 140°C (275°F) Gas 1 and simmer for 3 minutes for the sauce to bubble through. Serve with rice or noodles.

Australians and New Zealanders can trace their ancestors to almost every part of the world, so their casserole dishes reflect that multi-ethnic past, a veritable Cook's Tour of the globe. You find lamb ragouts from Greece, seafood soups from the Mediterranean and South-east Asia and beef braises from Britain.

The first settlers were English, Scots and Irish, so dishes from Britain form the basis of Antipodean cuisine. The face of Australian food was changed forever after World War II, when 'New Australians' came from Greece, Italy, the Lebanon, the Baltic States, Central and Eastern Europe and Jewish people from all over. The result was a plethora of new and vibrant ingredients and interesting cooking. Further change occurred with the post-1972 influx from the Middle East, Vietnam, Indonesia and other parts of South-east Asia. To the traditional stews and braises of Europe were added dishes like curry from Thailand, *pho* from Vietnam and *laksa* from Malaysia.

Australian cooks make use of incredible ingredients: beef and lamb that give new meaning to the words 'free range'; unusual local game such as kangaroo and buffalo; fish and seafood of extraordinary variety, freshness and quality; and fruits, vegetables and spices produced by farmers working in a huge range of climates. Added to that are the legendary wines of Australia and New Zealand – good to drink and very good for cooking.

This is an area where local cuisine is being constantly reborn, in a climate of absolute passion about food. All in all, this must be one of the most exciting places in the world to cook and eat today.

AUSTRALIA AND NEW ZEALAND

Australian Seafood Stew

All countries with a coastline develop their own traditional forms of fish stew and Australia is no exception. A marvellous variety of fish and seafood, plus a vibrant multi-ethnic tradition, make for a unique and fascinating version of this universal dish. There is a strong influence from South-east Asia, but the style is reminiscent of France's generous Bordeaux *fruits de mer* dishes. Monkfish is not caught in Australian waters, but its texture is very suited to fish stews: substitute any similar local fish with firm white flesh. Choose any combination of shellfish such as clams or mussels, plus crustacea such as prawns or lobsters. Just remember, don't cook any kind of seafood for very long, or it will be come tough and lose its flavour, while fish will disintegrate. Cook gently and only until the flesh becomes opaque.

Australian Seafood Stew

step-by-step

2 tablespoons peanut or sunflower oil

2 large onions, finely sliced

5 cm fresh ginger, finely chopped

3 large garlic cloves, crushed

2 stalks of lemongrass, very finely sliced

6 kaffir lime leaves or juice of 1 lime

250 ml white wine

about 1 kg mussels, well scrubbed, with beards removed

20 clams

1 litre fish stock

2 fresh red chillies, halved lengthways

4 small crayfish or lobster tails (optional)

500 g monkfish or other firm fish, skinned and cut into 3 cm chunks

8 large prawns

sea salt, to taste

TO SERVE

4 spring onions, sliced

2 red chillies, sliced

coriander leaves, torn

SERVES 4

1 Heat the oil in a wok or casserole, add the onion, ginger, garlic, lemongrass and kaffir lime leaves or lime juice and sauté until the onions are softened and translucent. Add the wine and 250 ml water and bring to the boil.

2 Add the mussels* and clams, put on the lid and steam until they open, shaking the pan from time to time.

*Make sure all the mussels have been scraped, rinsed and the beards pulled away and discarded before cooking. Tap the mussels against the kitchen counter and discard any that don't close. Clams should also close when tapped.

3 Remove the opened shellfish with a slotted spoon, put in a bowl and keep them warm. If they were very sandy, you may need to strain the cooking liquid, then return it to the pan. Add the stock and bring to the boil.

4 Add the chillies and crayfish or lobster tails, if using, and simmer until the shells change colour and the flesh is opaque all the way through (the time will depend on the size of the tails). When cooked, remove from the pan and cut in half lengthways. Add to the mussels and keep them warm.

5 Add the fish and prawns and poach gently until they are opaque all the way through – do not overcook or the prawns will be tough. Taste the liquid and adjust the seasoning. (Take care, because mussels are often salty and it's easy to add too much.)

6 Divide the seafood between 4 big soup bowls, bring the liquid to the boil, then ladle into the bowls.

7 Top with the spring onions, chillies and torn coriander leaves. Serve the stew with Chinese soup spoons and chopsticks, and a small dish of sliced chillies for people to help themselves.

Meat cooked on the bone has a very different texture from the boned type where the meat can shrink back unimpeded into a tight ball. The meat remains stretched as it cooks and has a tender, far more open texture.

Braised Lamb Shanks
with Orange and Marmalade

4 lamb shanks

4 tablespoons olive oil

3 garlic cloves, sliced

freshly squeezed juice of 2 oranges, about 250 ml

125 ml dry white wine

zest of 1 lemon, removed with a zester or potato peeler

3 tablespoons bitter orange marmalade

125 ml chicken stock (page 134) or water

sea salt and freshly ground black pepper

SERVES 4

Preheat an overhead grill until very hot. Brush the shanks with 3 tablespoons of the oil and season well, then grill, turning them as necessary until well browned all over.

Heat the remaining oil in a flameproof casserole, add the garlic and brown gently without burning. Add the shanks, orange juice, white wine and lemon zest. Bring to the boil on top of the stove, cover with a lid, then transfer to a preheated oven and cook at 180°C (350°F) Gas 4 for 1 hour, or until the meat pulls away from the bones.

Using a slotted spoon, transfer the shanks to a plate or bowl and keep them warm. Transfer the casserole to the top of the stove over a medium heat.

Add the marmalade to the casserole, stir until well blended, bring to the boil and simmer until the liquid has been reduced to a coating glaze.

Return the shanks to the casserole and turn in the glaze until well coated. Serve on heated dinner plates. Add the stock to the casserole, stir to scrape up the flavoured bits left in the pan, then spoon over the shanks and serve.

Oxtail makes a rich stew and is popular everywhere, especially in Australia, with its huge beef industry. Oxtail's natural gelatin gives the dish a delicious, sticky, glutinous texture. However, it also has an excessive amount of fat on the biggest sections, most of which must be cut away before cooking and lifted off when the cooking is complete. You can also chill the casserole overnight and remove the fat when cold.

Oxtail in Red Wine

7 tablespoons olive oil

3 tablespoons plain flour

2 large onions, sliced

2 oxtails, about 2 kg, jointed cleanly into sections, trimmed of fat

2 carrots, cut into chunks

4 tomatoes, chopped

2–3 sprigs of thyme

1 celery stalk, sliced

3 bay leaves

10 peppercorns

150 ml brandy

1 bottle red wine, 750 ml

1.75 litres beef stock (page 136)

sea salt and freshly ground black pepper

TO SERVE

freshly cooked vegetables, such as baby carrots, turnips and parsnips and green vegetables such as broccoli

mashed potatoes

SERVES 4–6

To make a roux, put 3 tablespoons of the oil in a small frying pan, add the flour and cook gently, stirring, until it becomes a nutty brown colour.

Heat another 3 tablespoons of the oil in a large, flameproof casserole, add the onion and sauté until golden. Add the smaller pieces of oxtail, carrots, tomatoes, thyme, celery, bay leaves and peppercorns. Fry until browned. Transfer to a bowl and keep everything warm.

Rinse the casserole, return to the heat and add the remaining oil. Add the larger pieces of oxtail and fry until browned on all sides. Pour off the fat.

Warm the brandy in a small saucepan, light with a match and pour over the meat. Shake the casserole gently, keeping the flame alight as long as possible to burn off all the alcohol.

Transfer the meat to the bowl of vegetables and add the wine to the casserole. Bring to the boil and cook until it becomes syrupy and almost disappears. Stir in the roux, then the stock. Bring to the boil, stirring all the time to make a sauce. Add salt and pepper, then gently mix in all the meat and vegetables. Transfer to a preheated oven and cook at 150°C (300°F) Gas 2 for at least 3 hours, or until the meat is falling off the bone.

Remove from the oven and set aside for about 10 minutes to let the fat rise to the surface. Spoon off as much fat as you can. Alternatively, let cool, then chill overnight.

About 1 hour before serving, remove any fat from the surface and reheat the stew, adding a little boiling water if the sauce has become too dry. Taste and adjust the seasoning. Transfer the large pieces of meat to a bowl and strain the gravy over. Discard the vegetables and any small bones.

Gently return the stew to the casserole and top with your choice of freshly cooked vegetables. Serve with lots of mashed potatoes for mopping up the sauce.

It may seem odd to find Vietnamese food as an example of casserole cooking in Australia, especially with French bread, but Vietnamese immigrants have had an exciting effect on food Down Under. In addition, their baking prowess is a legacy of the French colonial period and they have opened some of Australia's best bread bakeries. This beef casserole is eaten as street food or at home – served with crusty French sticks or rice.

Vietnamese Beef with Baguettes

1 stalk of lemongrass, peeled and finely chopped

leaves from 3 sprigs of mint, chopped

2 tablespoons fish sauce

1 teaspoon brown sugar

3 cm fresh ginger, peeled and grated

1 red chilli, deseeded and chopped

2 garlic cloves, crushed

freshly ground black pepper

1 kg boneless beef (shin or chuck), cut into 2.5 cm cubes

about 2 tablespoons peanut oil

2 tablespoons tomato purée

3 tomatoes, skinned, deseeded and chopped, about 500 g

1 litre water or Vietnamese Beef Stock (page 139)

TO SERVE

6 spring onions, shredded

sprigs of mint

crusty baguettes

SERVES 4–6

Put the lemongrass, mint, fish sauce, sugar, ginger, chilli, garlic and lots of freshly ground black pepper in a bowl and mix well.

Add the beef and turn to coat. Cover and marinate in the refrigerator for about 2 hours or overnight.

Heat the oil in a casserole dish, then add the beef in batches and fry until browned on all sides. Using a slotted spoon, remove each batch to a plate and keep it warm while you cook the remainder.

Return all the beef to the pan, add the tomato purée and tomatoes and cook for 3–4 minutes until they start to break down. Add 1 litre water and bring to the boil. Reduce the heat and simmer for about 2 hours until the meat is spoon-tender and the sauce rich but not too thick.

Serve in small bowls, topped with shredded spring onion and mint sprigs, accompanied by crusty baguettes for mopping up the juices.

The original of this chicken dish came from a gourmet food writer in Melbourne twenty-five years ago and the cook-in sauce seemed then to be well ahead of its time. Nowadays, it is more normal to mix Western ingredients (Italian olives, pimento and basil) and Eastern (soy sauce, lemon and honey) to make a fusion whole. Sometimes fusions don't work, but this one does, and it's typical of the culinary cross-pollination that happens in Australia and New Zealand. The sweet potato base mops up all the cooking juices from the chicken.

Chicken and Sweet Potatoes
with Honey, Soy and Lemon

6 tablespoons olive oil

2 sweet potatoes, about 1 kg, cut into 1 cm rounds

4 chicken legs (thighs and drumsticks)

1 cup pimento-stuffed green olives

125 ml dry white wine

4 tablespoons honey

2 cups basil leaves

6 crushed garlic

4 tablespoons soy sauce

finely grated zest and juice of 2 lemons

SERVES 4

Heat 4 tablespoons of the oil in a large frying pan, add the sweet potatoes and sauté until lightly browned. Transfer to an ovenproof casserole.

Add the remaining oil to the frying pan, add the chicken legs and sauté until browned all over. Put them on top of the sweet potatoes in the casserole.

Put the olives, wine, honey, basil, garlic, soy sauce, lemon zest and juice into a food processor or blender and purée until smooth. Pour the mixture over the chicken.

Transfer to a preheated oven and cook at 200°C (400°F) Gas 6 for about 30 minutes, or until the casserole comes to the boil, then reduce the heat to 150°C (300°F) Gas 2 and simmer for 30 minutes, or until the chicken is tender.

Capsicum Chilli Tian
with Goats' Cheese and Chorizo

This Antipodean version of a Provençal tian is cooked in a wide, shallow, open casserole dish. Peppers are called 'capsicums' in Australia, which is the correct name for this whole group of vegetables, including chillies.

4 red peppers (capsicums)

2 yellow or orange peppers (capsicums)

2 red onions, finely chopped

125 ml extra virgin olive oil, plus extra for brushing and drizzling

2 small mild chorizo sausages, finely sliced

a handful of basil leaves

16 cherry tomatoes, halved

1–2 medium-hot fresh red chillies, deseeded and finely sliced (optional)

about 250 g mature goats' cheese, cut into 12 chunks

sea salt flakes and freshly ground black pepper

PESTO
1 large bunch of fresh basil

a large handful of parsley leaves

75 ml olive oil

4 tablespoons pine nuts, about 25 g

2 garlic cloves, crushed

75 g grated Parmesan cheese

TO SERVE
salad leaves

sprigs of basil

lemon wedges

char-grilled Italian bread

SERVES 4

To make the pesto, put the basil, parsley, olive oil, pine nuts and garlic in a blender and process until smooth. Add the Parmesan, then blend again.

Cut the peppers in half lengthways through the stalk. Carefully remove the cores.

Put the peppers in a plastic bag, add the 125 ml olive oil, salt and pepper, then shake until well coated with oil.

Brush a shallow tian or casserole dish with extra olive oil and add the peppers, cut side up, cramming them close together. Put a slice of chorizo, a basil leaf, a halved cherry tomato, a spoonful of pesto, some onion, a little chilli, if using, and a chunk of goats' cheese in each pepper half. Drizzle more olive oil over the top.

Cook in a preheated oven at 200°C (400°F) Gas 6 for 30 minutes, or until all the peppers are tender and crispy brown at the edges and the cheese is melted and bubbling.

Serve on small plates with a tangle of salad leaves, extra fresh basil leaves scattered over the top and wedges of lemon for squeezing. Char-grilled Italian bread is perfect for mopping up the delicious juices.

Basic Preparations

Some useful basic principles of casserole cooking found in many cuisines include:

Browning onions

Onions contain natural sugars. When heated to a high temperature, those sugars start to turn brown and develop delicious caramel flavour and colour, just like loose sugar. This adds considerably to the quality of flavour and appearance of stocks and casseroles. Over-browning produces a bitter taste.

Browning meats

Always brown meat in batches. Why? Because when meat is fried, the fibres shrink and squeeze out the meat juices. These in turn form a concentrated meat 'glace' or glaze. However, if the source of heat is not strong enough to reduce the liquid as it appears, it collects in the pan, boiling and toughening the meat. The answer is to brown the meat in smaller batches and use the largest pan practicable so that boiling doesn't occur.

Thickening

Wheat flour

Flour is used in sauces and gravies to thicken the liquid. Mixed in equal quantities with butter, oil or fat, it is called 'manié'. When this mixture is cooked, it is called a roux and loses its raw, floury taste. With longer cooking, the roux turns brown – as in many Cajun recipes – and loses some of its thickening properties. This last browning must be done very slowly so that the flour colours evenly, otherwise it will 'catch' and burn in places.

Cornflour, rice flour and potato flour

These starches do not contain the gluten of wheat. In casserole cooking, they have several advantages:

• Their thickening process leaves a clearer sauce.
• They absorb fats floating on the surface of liquids.
• They thicken to a maximum just below boiling point, but should preferably be boiled to achieve the best flavour.

Cooking with wines and spirits, alcohols and vinegars

These are among the best flavouring agents found in the cook's store cupboard. They are acidulators with preservative qualities.

The correct way to use them is to boil off their unwanted esters and concentrate their flavours. This is usually done when a recipe requires a pan to be 'deglazed' in wine, spirits or vinegar. The result is that any fried particles or meat juices are dissolved into the deglazing liquid and flavours retained.

Beer often needs sugar added to counteract its bitterness.

Vegetable Stock

Vegetable stock should be made with a range of vegetables to produce a clear, clean liquid, full of flavour. The choice of ingredients is crucial – avoid starchy vegetables like potatoes and parsnips, which will cloud the stock, and those with flavour too dominating, such as the cabbage family. Wine is acid and counteracts the sweetness of cooked onions: it also clears the stock. I sometimes add a garlic clove and a twist of tangerine or orange peel with a small bunch of lemon thyme for the last ten minutes, to lift the flavour out of the ordinary, but these are optional. Don't add salt to stock – add it to the dish as required.

Cooking with spices

Spices are used as flavourings and preservatives and, preferably, should be ground (like coffee beans) just before use. Roasting them in a dry pan or in fat or oil releases their aromas and matures their flavour. A mixture of spices is known in India as a 'masala' and great care is taken to create special combinations suited to each dish.

In many South-east Asian cuisines, the spices are usually ground into pastes using a mortar and pestle (a modern coffee grinder kept for the purpose is a good lazy-cook's substitute). The spice pastes are then fried in oil or in a small amount of coconut cream to release their aromas before the rest of the ingredients are added.

Saffron, whether powder or threads, is usually lightly toasted, then ground or steeped in water to draw out its flavour and colour. This will take several hours and should be done before being added to the dish.

2 tomatoes,

1 leek, white part only

1 carrot

1 onion

2 shallots

a bouquet garni (a bundle of herbs, tied up with kitchen string)

10 peppercorns

125 ml white wine

MAKES 750 ML

Wash the vegetables (peeling is optional). Chop them coarsely and put everything into a large non-reactive (stainless steel or enamel) stockpot. Cover with about 1.25 litres water and add the wine. Simmer for 2 hours and then bring to a rolling boil for a few moments. Strain through a fine sieve or muslin. Chill and freeze.

Alternatively, for a different flavour, heat a little oil in the pan first, then fry the vegetables until their sugar caramelizes and they brown. Do not let the onions become too dark, or their sugar will burn and give a bitter taste. This stock tends to be a bit cloudy.

Microwave Stock

I have made a similar stock in the microwave, using less water and at a LOW power: it took about half the time.

Chicken Stock

It is always a good thing to have chicken stock available as it has so many applications, ranging from aspics to soups and casseroles, and will never be wasted. This method will produce an excellent white stock, as neither the vegetables nor the meats and bones have been browned. The optional wine or vinegar helps coagulate the loose proteins, making them easier to strain out.

Clarifying stocks

Really sparklingly clear stocks are usually reserved for making consommés or aspics, as a little sediment does no harm to sauces thickened with flours or other liaisons. However, with some Asian dishes, a beautifully clear stock is called for and then the care must start right from the beginning as a fatty, opaque stock cannot be rectified – or almost never. Follow steps 1–4 here, then pass the liquid through a fine strainer or muslin. Put 150 g totally lean, finely hand-chopped meat, chicken or fish (according to the stock being cleared) in a bowl, then add 3 lightly whisked egg whites for every 2–2.5 litres stock. Heat the stock just to boiling point, stir in the egg white mixture and let it simmer for 30 minutes without disturbing it other than by opening a small blowhole to release steam build-up. During this time, any floating impurities rise to the surface and stick to the albumen in the egg white, which cooks into a solid mat. Carefully remove the mat, then pour the clear liquid underneath through a muslin-lined sieve into a bowl.

2 carcasses uncooked chicken, 1 kg wings or 1 turkey drumstick, sliced

any giblets or trimmings such as wingtips from the chickens

4 carrots, sliced

1 leek, well cleaned and sliced

1 onion, sliced or chopped

1 celery stalk

1 teaspoon black peppercorns

1 bay leaf

1 sprig of thyme

2–3 parsley stalks

2 tablespoons white wine or 1 tablespoon white wine vinegar

75 g unsalted butter (optional)

MAKES 1.5 LITRES

1 Chop the chicken carcasses into several large pieces, put into a stockpot with any giblets or trimmings, cover with cold water and skim off any fat that rises to the surface. Bring to a gentle simmer without boiling and skim off any foam that rises to the surface.

2 Add all the prepared vegetables, herbs, peppercorns and white wine or white wine vinegar, return to simmering and cook for 1½ hours.

Alternatively, heat the butter, if using, in a frying pan, add the vegetables and cook until lightly browned. Add the chicken and proceed as before.

White Stock

A classic white stock contains a variety of meat and bones. Veal and veal bones are preferred ingredients. Should a boiling fowl be available, it gives a most flavourful stock, but it needs to be de-fatted thoroughly (see the method for Asian Chicken Stock, page 138). If unavailable, use plenty of raw chicken wings or wingtips and carcasses if available or a turkey drumstick. A pig's trotter will produce the necessary gelatin in the absence of veal bones, but enough chicken bones will also do the trick. Some trimmings from pork or lamb are acceptable, but not in any great proportion to the rest of the bones because the stock produced from these tastes a little sweet. Beef trimmings are excellent. The method is the same as for chicken stock.

3 Strain the stock through a sieve.

Note For a clearer stock, strain through muslin (although this will take longer).

4 Chicken fat will not solidify at normal refrigerator temperature. Cool the stock quickly, then freeze. After 3–4 hours, the solidified fat can be scraped off with a spoon. Return the stock to the pan, bring to the boil and simmer until reduced to the required intensity of flavour. Freeze in conveniently sized containers.

Slow Cooker Stock

A slow cooker is a convenient way to make stock. Put the raw chicken carcasses in a slow cooker without any vegetables, cover with cold water and a lid, switch onto the higher setting and cook for at least 8 hours or overnight. Strain, cool and freeze. Scrape off all the fat and bring to the boil to reduce, if necessary, to about 1 litre.

Beef Stock

When the sugars in the meats, bones or vegetables are caramelized through roasting or frying, the result is what is known as a 'brown stock'. It has a richer colour and a little more flavour. As with all stock making, there are a few basic rules:

• Never continue boiling a stock once it has reached the boil. Just keep it hot enough for the steam to find a blowhole in the fat and puff gently through. The reason is that, as the fat dissolves and floats to the surface, it makes a transparent layer on the top. If this is broken up continually by lots of bubbles breaking the surface, the fat is drawn back down into the body of the stock, where it gradually combines and emulsifies with the liquid, producing an opaque and fatty stock. A little boiling at the beginning doesn't hurt, but a vigorous one halfway through is not good at all.

• Use rib bones, not marrow bones as are usually recommended – marrow bones will make the stock fatty.

• Never add salt to a stock – keep the salt for the final dish.

5 kg mixed beef bones (see left)

1 kg shin of beef and beef trimmings (optional)

1 kg onions, coarsely chopped

1 kg carrots, cut into chunks

1 large leek, split, well washed and drained, then thickly sliced

2 tomatoes, halved

a bouquet garni (a bundle of herbs tied up with kitchen string)

150 ml red wine or wine vinegar

MAKES 1–1.5 LITRES

1 Put the bones in 2 roasting tins and roast in a preheated oven at 200°C (400°F) Gas 6 for 25 minutes – they should brown slowly.

2 Add the vegetables and increase the oven heat as high as it will go, or 250°C (500°F) Gas 10, to caramelize the juices left in the tin and brown the vegetables, about 5 minutes. Do not let the bones char or blacken.

3 When the bones and vegetables are nicely browned, transfer them to a stockpot, add the bouquet garni, cover with cold water and bring to the boil.

4 Pour off any fat left in the roasting tins, add the wine or vinegar and boil until reduced by two-thirds. Mix in 250 ml water and pour into the stockpot. The acid helps coagulate the albumin that forms as foam on top of the liquid and should be skimmed off. Simmer, uncovered, for about 4 hours, making sure the liquid does not boil.

5 Strain the stock into a bowl. Discard the bones and vegetables. If you pour it through muslin, the stock will be clearer, but it will take longer. If the pot has a tap, drain off most of the stock, being careful to leave behind the fat which is lying on the surface. To cool the stock quickly, put the bowl into a sink of iced water.

6 Chill the stock for about 4 hours or overnight. It will form a lid of fat which can be lifted off and discarded. Return the stock to the pot, bring to the boil and reduce to strengthen the flavour. Cool, divide into small containers (about 250 ml) and store in the refrigerator or freeze. To make a glace, reduce still further until syrupy.

Asian Stocks

Casserole recipes in some parts of the world, such as the Middle East and India, are usually made with water instead of stock as their poaching liquid. In East and South-east Asia, however, a wide range of stocks is used to add flavour, or even as the main ingredient in curries and soups, especially light soups with quick-cooking seafood, vegetables or noodles. Flavour and clarity are prized – in the first recipe, you will find an excellent technique for clarifying stock.

Asian Chicken Stock

A delicious light chicken stock of very good quality – fat free and very clear.

1 kg chicken carcasses, wings or wingtips
5 cm fresh ginger, sliced
250 g shallots or large-bulbed spring onions
8 garlic cloves, lightly crushed
10 peppercorns
6 coriander stalks with leaves

MAKES ABOUT 1.5 LITRES

Remove and discard all fat from the carcasses and chop roughly. Put into a large, stainless steel or enamel saucepan. Add 3 litres cold water. Heat to simmering, but do not let boil. Skim any foam off the surface. Add the other ingredients, heat to simmering point, letting the surface break with slow bubbles in several places to release the steam.

Simmer for about 2½ hours. Drain off the liquid – which should still be clear – through a muslin-lined sieve into a bowl. Cool, then freeze until the fat has congealed on the surface.

Scrape off the fat and discard. While the liquid is frozen, tilt the bowl and pour a little boiling water over the surface to wash off any fat still clinging to it or to the sides of the bowl. Transfer the stock into a clean saucepan, bring to a rolling boil and reduce to 1.5 litres, or until the strength is to your liking. Use immediately or freeze in convenient quantities.

Thai-style Stock

This simple stock can be made with all chicken or chicken and pork. Use it as a basis for soups and curries.

about 1.5 kg chicken carcasses, chopped into 4–6 pieces, or wings

about 500 g lean pork with bones, cut into large chunks

a handful of coriander, with stalks and roots if possible

a large pinch of salt

MAKES ABOUT 1 LITRE

Put the chicken, pork and coriander in a large saucepan, then add the salt and about 2 litres water. Bring to the boil and skim off any foam that rises to the surface. Repeat the skimming several times, then reduce the heat to a gentle simmer and cook for about 1 hour.

Remove from the heat and let cool. When cool, pour gently through a fine sieve, so as not to disturb too much of the sediment. Discard the bones and sediment.

Chill, preferably overnight, then scrape off the fat from the top of the stock.

Use immediately or freeze in convenient quantities.

South-east Asian Chicken or Pork Stock

A basic stock made from any available poultry or meat. The sugar-salt-spice combination is very common in Vietnam. When the stock is strained, reserve any small pieces of meat or chicken and use them in sandwiches or salads.

2 kg chicken carcasses or pork bones, or a combination of both

3 cm fresh ginger, peeled and sliced

1 shallot or onion, cut into wedges

a large pinch of salt

a pinch of sugar

MAKES ABOUT 1.5 LITRES

Put the bones in a large saucepan and cover with cold water.

Bring slowly to the boil, then boil for 10–15 minutes, skimming off the foam several times.

Reduce the heat, add the ginger, shallot or onion, salt and sugar, then simmer for about 2 hours.

Carefully strain through a fine sieve, discarding the bones, flavourings and sediment. Pick off and reserve any shreds of meat. Chill and remove the fat. Use immediately or freeze in convenient quantities.

Vietnamese Beef Stock

The basis of the legendary Vietnamese beef noodle soup, *pho bo*, and of many other soups, this is a useful stock.

1 kg shin of beef, with bones, cut into 3 cm slices

500 g stewing beef, in the piece

3 cm fresh ginger, peeled and sliced

a pinch of salt

3 tablespoons fish sauce

2 whole star anise

1 cinnamon stick, broken

2 onions, sliced

MAKES ABOUT 1 LITRE

Put the bones in a large saucepan, cover completely with cold water and bring to the boil. Boil for 15 minutes, skimming off the foam every few minutes. When the foam stops rising, reduce the heat, add the stewing beef and simmer for about 2 hours.

Add the ginger, salt, fish sauce, star anise, cinnamon stick and onions and continue simmering for 30 minutes.

Carefully strain through a fine sieve, discarding the bones, flavourings and sediment. Reserve the meat for another dish. Chill, remove the fat and use the stock within 3 days or freeze in convenient quantities.

Fish Stock

The best fish bones are those from flat fish such as turbot, plaice, sole and halibut. Non-oily round fish bones from cod, monk or skate may be used, but do not use oily fish such as mackerel, trout, salmon, sardines, pilchards or any smoked fish such as smoked cod or haddock. If you wish to use salmon bones for a salmon-flavoured stock, before using it you must skim off any globules of orange-coloured oil floating on the surface. Use fish stocks as soon as possible because the flavour will deteriorate under refrigeration.

5 kg non-oily fish bones
75 g butter
2 onions, chopped
3 celery stalks, chopped
10 parsley stalks
10 peppercorns
1 bouquet garni
300 ml white wine

MAKES 2 LITRES

Pick over the bones and discard any gut or oily fish. Soak and rinse, or run water over them until no blood is visible.

Meanwhile, heat the butter in a large, stainless steel or enamel stockpot, add the vegetables and herbs and sauté gently for about 5 minutes. On no account let them brown.

Add the wine and bring to the boil. Add the drained fish bones. Cover with iced water and ice cubes if you have them, then skim off and discard the fat that congeals on the surface. Bring to a gentle simmer and cook for 30 minutes.

Strain into a bowl and allow to settle. Pour off the clear stock into a clean pan, discarding any residue. Boil to reduce the stock to about 2 litres, or until the flavour is as strong as you need. Transfer to convenient containers, about 250 ml each, then freeze.

Notes

• When making fish stock, never let the bones boil for more than 30 seconds, or they begin to dissolve their gelatin and the stock will become tacky when it is reduced to strengthen flavour.

• Sauté the vegetables in a little butter first to part cook them or they will not give up their flavour as quickly as the fish.

• When the vegetables and bones are covered with iced water, the frying fat floats to the surface, solidifies and can be lifted off and discarded. Ice cubes will make sure the water is cold enough to congeal the butter.

• Never add shellfish to an ordinary fish stock because you don't know who might be allergic to them. Keep a separate shellfish stock made from mussels, scallop trimmings or the cooking water from lobsters or prawns.

Safety Considerations

If casseroles are to be stored and reheated after cooking, this should be done carefully. The conditions in which food poisoning may occur are:

• When precooked food contains organisms, such as the staphylococcus organisms, which generate poisons.

• When cross-contamination occurs and food acquires harmful organisms transferred to it from unsterilized utensils, boards and raw foods – the salmonella organisms.

The safest way to avoid food poisoning is to cook food from raw and then eat it right away whilst it is virtually sterilized. The elderly and very young should ideally be fed in this way, as their resistance to harmful bacteria tends to be low. However, with due care and attention to preventative procedures, there should be no problem with storing and reheating foods.

We ingest thousands of bacteria every day – some good, some bad – but trouble comes when we eat more of them than we can cope with over a short period.

There are two main situations in which this can occur. One is when food has been precooked, then kept in a warm environment: the other is when it has come into contact with dirty utensils or raw foods (which cannot be sterile), then left where the organisms can multiply.

Rule 1. Cooling

Cooked food should be cooled as soon as possible if it is not to be eaten immediately.

The cooking container should be lowered into a sink of iced water to reduce the temperature of the contents, especially stocks, as quickly as possible. This will reduce the length of time the contents are at a vulnerable temperature, typically between 70°C (about scalding point) and 4°C (the temperature of a cold refrigerator). There is an especially dangerous period at about 30°C (the temperature of a kitchen on a warm day) when bacteria, having landed on the cooked food, begin multiplying at an astonishing rate, doubling in number every few minutes. Dishes containing an amount of sugar or acid substances have a certain resistance to the problem, but are by no means immune.

Never put hot food in the freezer to cool quickly: this raises the temperature of the freezer and defrosts already frozen food.

Rule 2. Refrigerating

Once cool, stocks and meats should be covered and kept, for no more than 2 days, at or below 4°C – the recommended interior temperature for a domestic refrigerator – unless other forms of preservative have been employed.

After this time, meats and casseroles should be reheated and eaten. One of the bonus points here is that many casseroles benefit from this period of resting when flavours in the meats and liquids become interchanged and integrate into a more delectable whole.

The fat layer on stocks (other than poultry stocks, which have to be deep frozen) congeals at this temperature and may be lifted or scraped off prior to the stock being reduced.

Rule 3. Reheating

The temperature of wholesome food should be brought gently but steadily to a minimum 85°C all through if it is to be consumed immediately, and 100°C (boiling point) for 3 minutes when sterilizing stocks.

If the food is wholesome to be eaten cold, it will be wholesome when hot, if consumed at once. So, when you are reheating refrigerated food to eat immediately, there is no need to sterilize it. This may prevent overcooking, but will not guarantee to kill any salmonella present. However, if it has been stored correctly, there should not be sufficient numbers present to worry anybody but the very young or very old.

After this, food should preferably be discarded. Please note that cooked food that is not wholesome when eaten cold will not be wholesome just because it has been sterilized. The staphylococci organisms excrete poisons which are harmful and present in food even when boiled. Luckily, salmonella is killed at boiling point and rendered harmless.

Rule 4. Freezing

Only freeze raw meats, poultry, fish and vegetables and freshly cooked foods, stocks and leftovers.

NEVER be tempted to think that freezing will preserve a questionable casserole or stock, or one that's been refrigerated for too long.

From this low temperature, the time taken to reheat it will give ample time for bacteria to multiply and become really poisonous. Apart from keeping cooked food for too long in a warm atmosphere, this is the most dangerous situation in which bacteria can multiply and excrete poison.

It is a good idea to divide stews and casseroles into manageable quantities of 2, 4 or 6 portions, as is convenient for your own requirements. This will prevent either wastage or the temptation to refreeze once-frozen items.

At freezer temperatures, evaporation of moisture still takes place, producing after an appreciable time a condition called 'freezer burn' if items are not well wrapped or hermetically sealed. This is not poisonous, it just makes the food unpalatable and the burnt part should be cut away and discarded.

Certain foods, especially carbohydrates such as cooked rice, wheat flour and potatoes, do not freeze well. Some raw meats and fish containing a lot of water in their cells also do not freeze well.

This is because water expands just below freezing point and breaks the cell walls, which deflate and release their water on thawing – a pity, but not poisonous. Sometimes, stirring the offending water into the gravy will help overcome the fault. Commercial blast freezing prevents this problem, but home freezers do not.

Casseroles and stocks should not be kept in a freezer for more than 4–5 months. After this time, the flavour and appearance deteriorate, although they will continue to be safe to eat.

Rule 5. Thawing

Cooked food should be given enough time to thaw completely in a cool place or refrigerator or microwave before being reheated. Stocks should be boiled from frozen.

Microwaving may speed things up, but you should make sure the centre of the casserole reaches the required temperature before serving or before being finished off in a conventional oven. (Personally, I find this difficult to do without overcooking the outside.)

Index